Elizabeth James

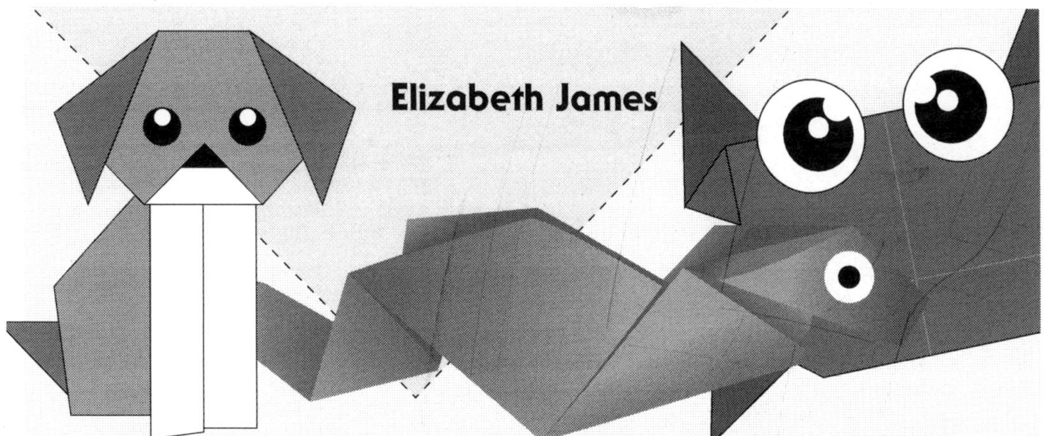

The Great Big Easy ORIGAMI Book for Boys

First published in 2016 by Kyle Craig Publishing

Copyright © 2016 Kyle Craig Publishing

Design: Julie Anson, Alison McNicol, Shutterstock, Inc.

ISBN: 978-1-78595-282-1

A CIP record for this book is available from the British Library.

A Kyle Craig Publication

www.kyle-craig.com

All Rights Reserved.

No part of this publication may be reproduced, stored in a retrieval system or transmitted by any form or by any means, electronic, recording or otherwise without the prior permission in writing from the publishers.

Unauthorised reproduction of any part of this publication by any means including photocopying is an infringement of copyright.

Welcome!

Welcome to your EASY ORIGAMI Book!

Origami is the traditional Japanese art of PAPER FOLDING, and is such a fun way to make cool animals and items out of a simple square of paper. Start with the easiest projects and work your way towards the more detailed ones as your origami skills increase!

– Origami Paper Pages Included!

At the rear of the book are some cool patterned pages that you can use as origami paper.

All the designs in this book start with a square piece of paper, so cut out the square of patterned paper and you're ready to go!

We have also included lots of cool eyes and animal noses and faces – try cutting these out and adding to your origami animal for a fun finish!!

Have Fun!

Origami Folding Symbols

Fold

Fold towards this direction

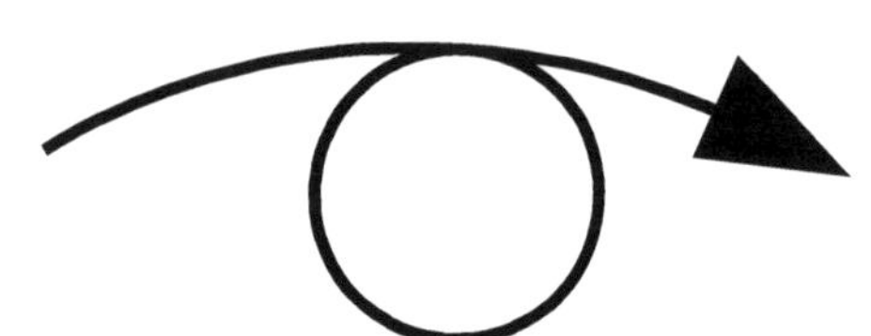

Fold, then unfold, to crease

Flip over

Push

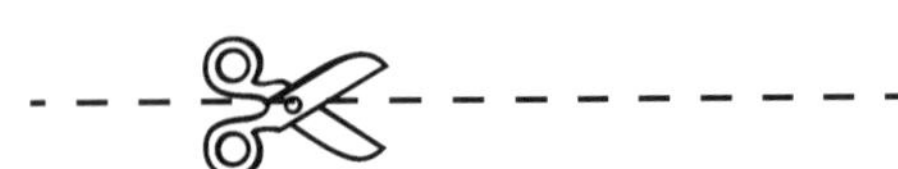

Cut here

Paper Plane

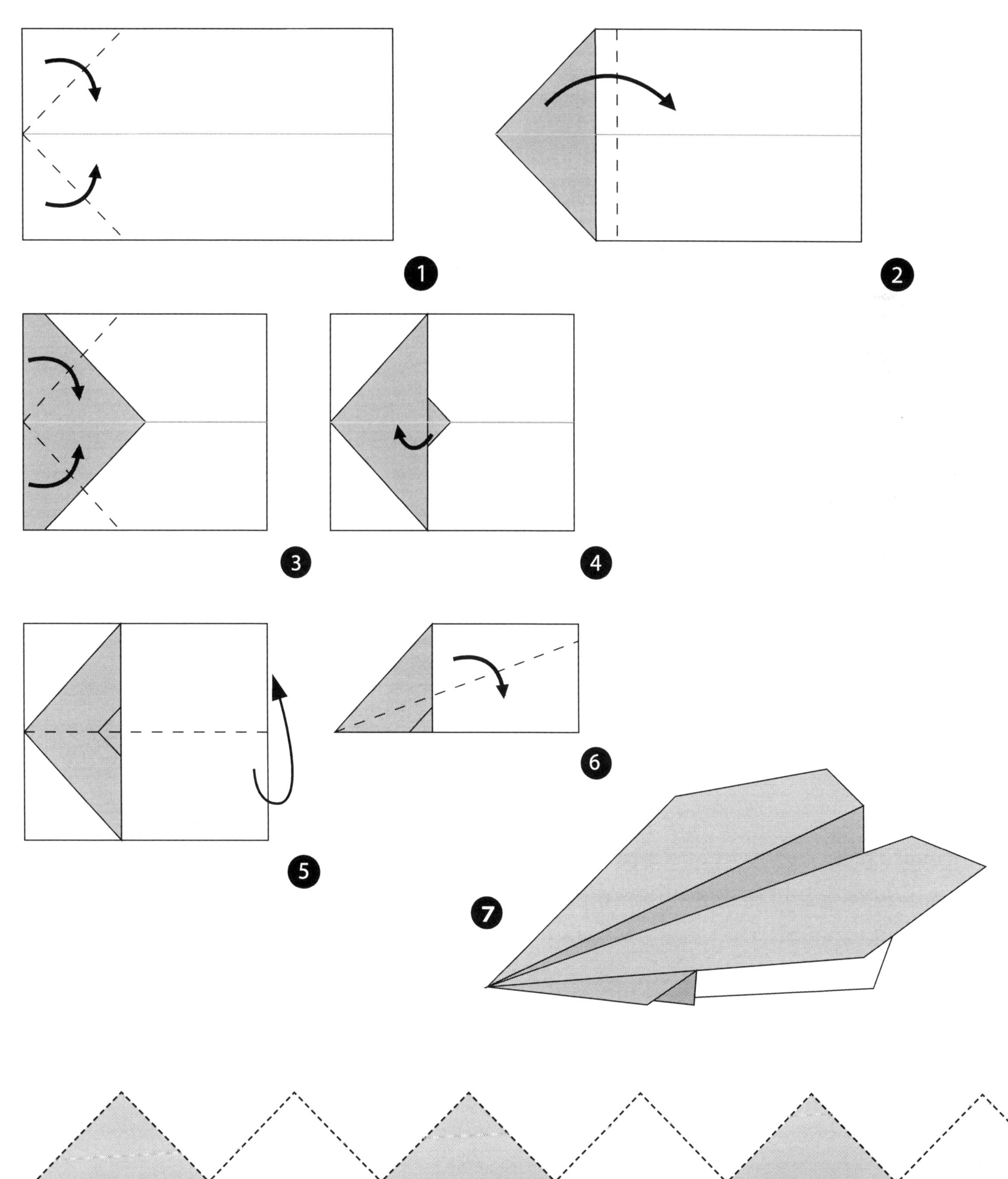

Giraffe

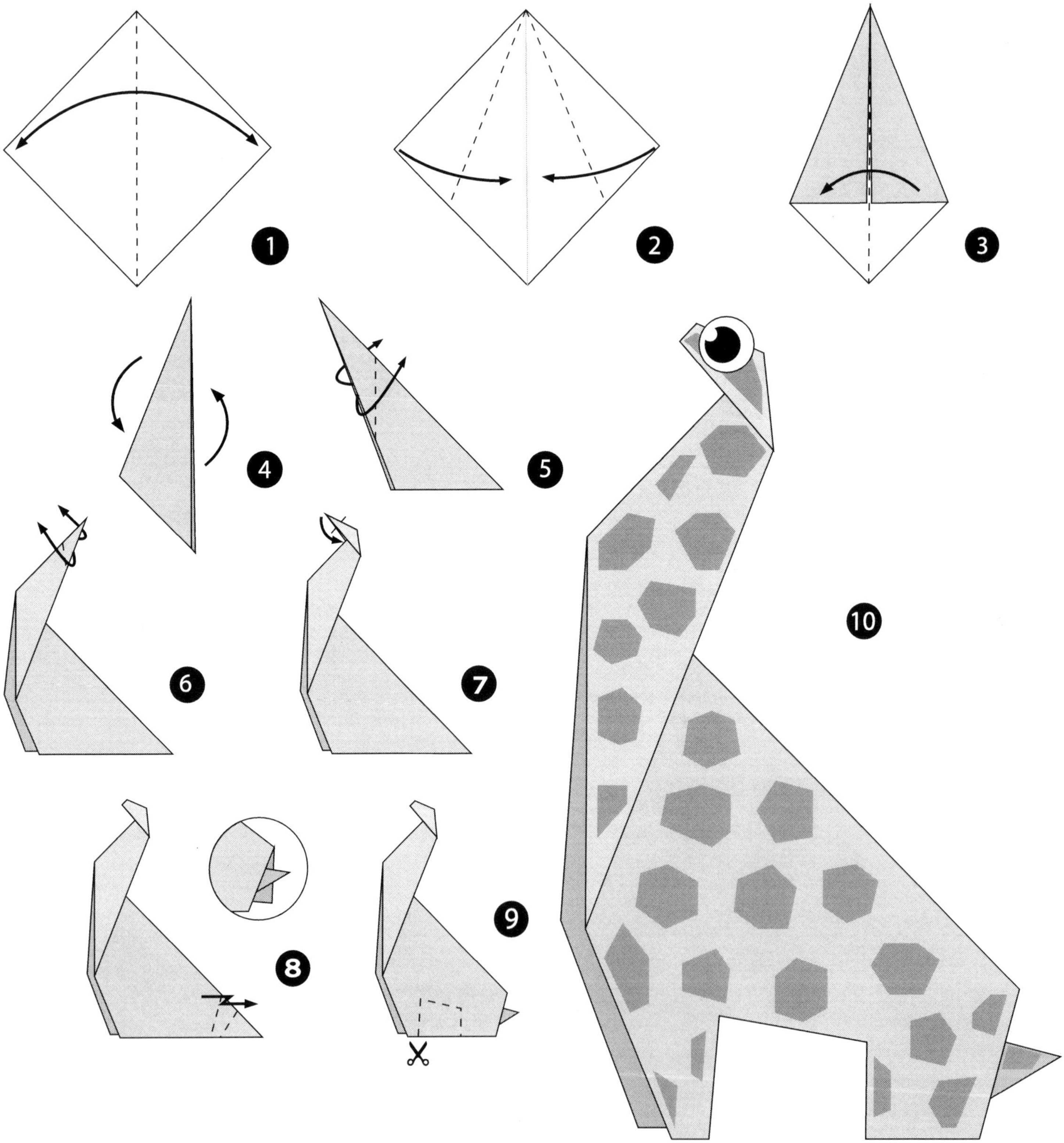

1

2

3

4

5

6

7

8

9

10

Car

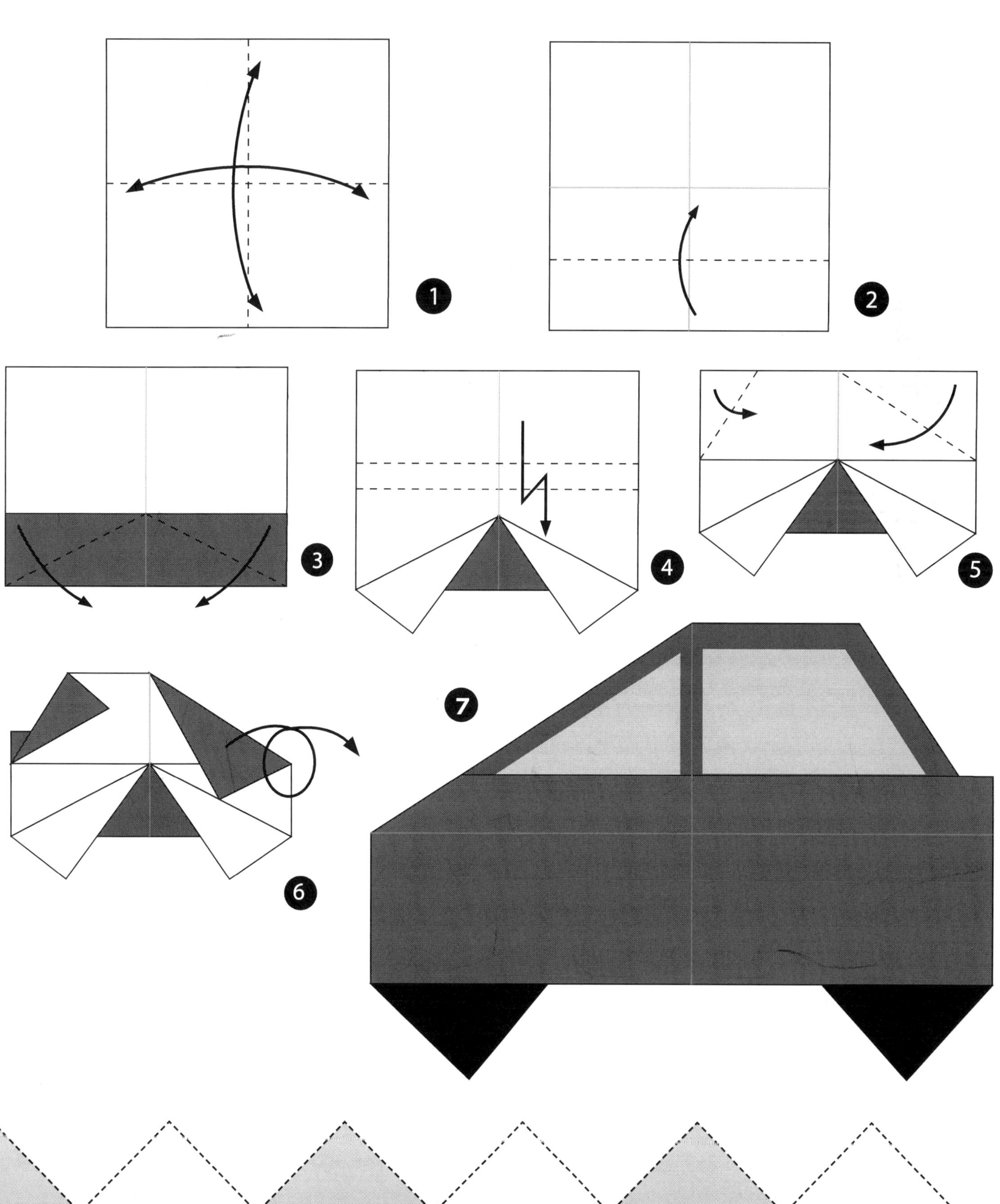

Tyrannosuarus

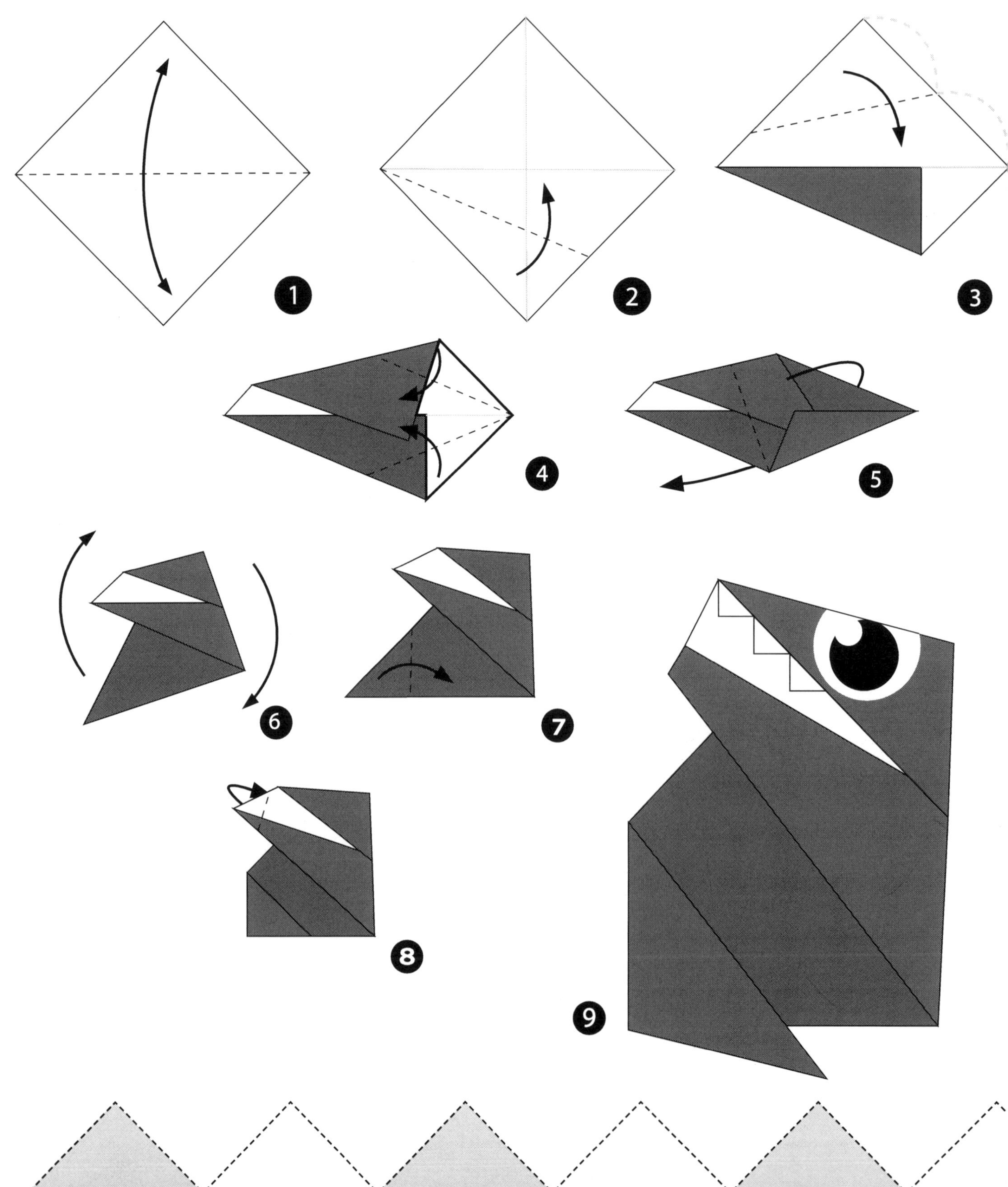

Worm

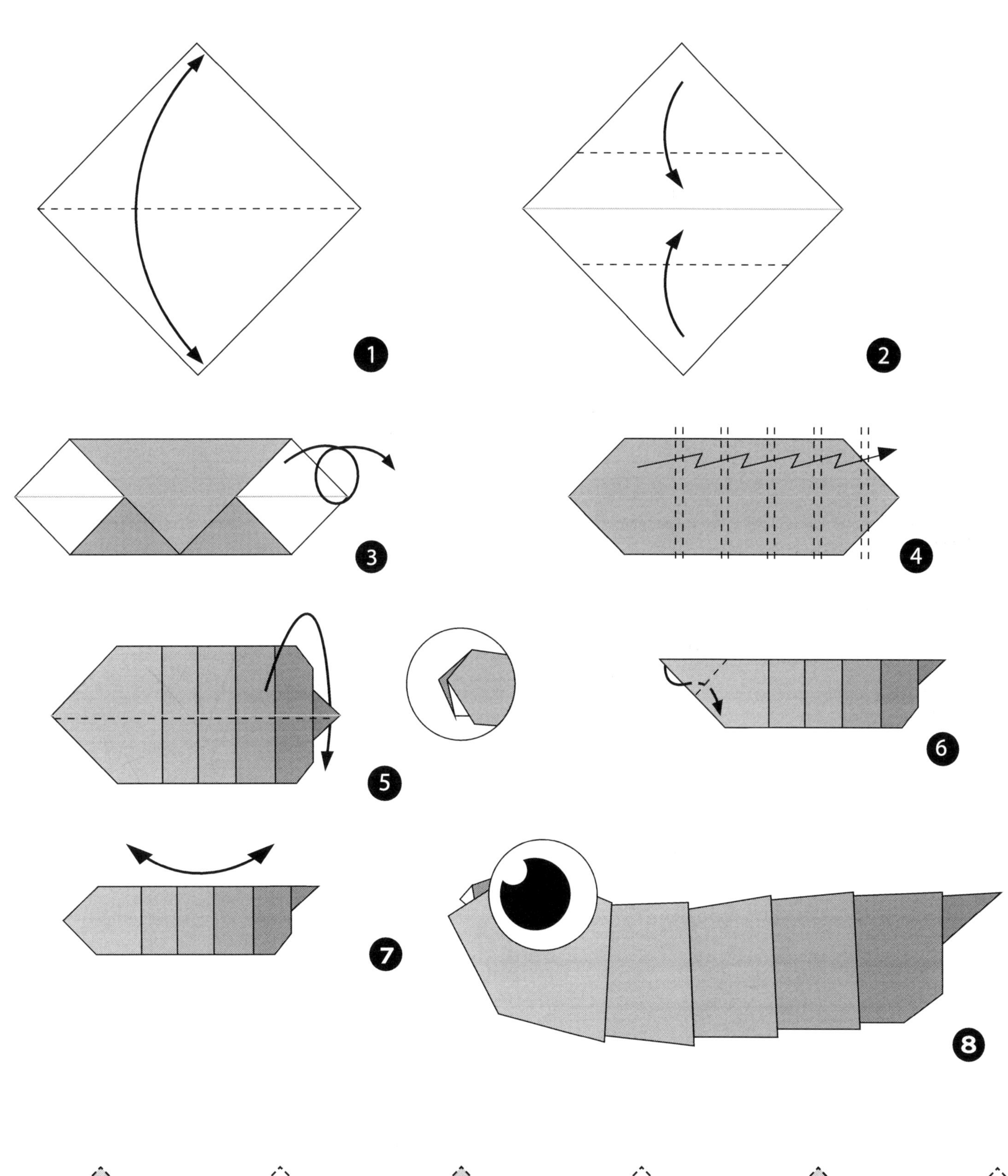

Garbage Bin

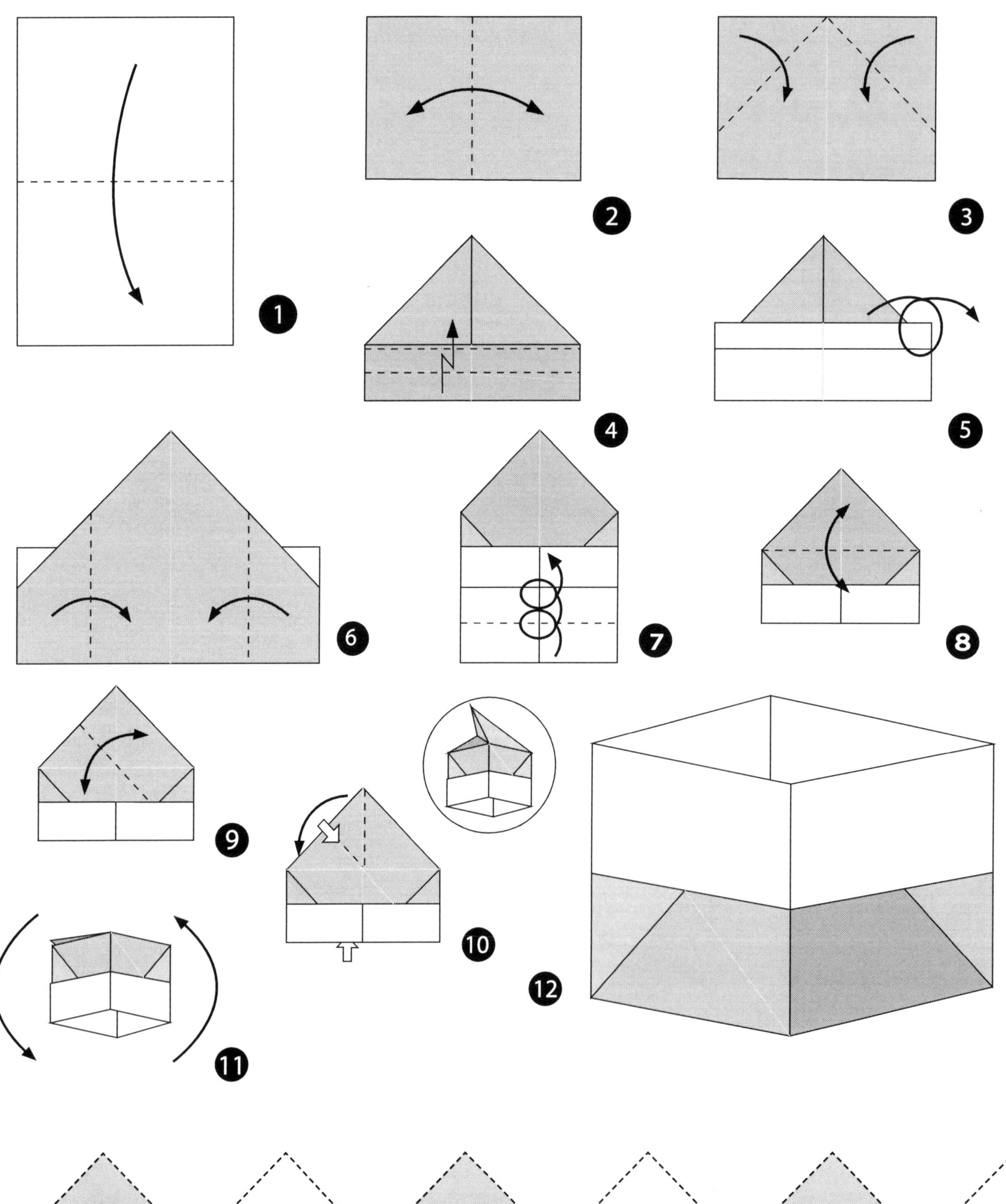

Dolphin

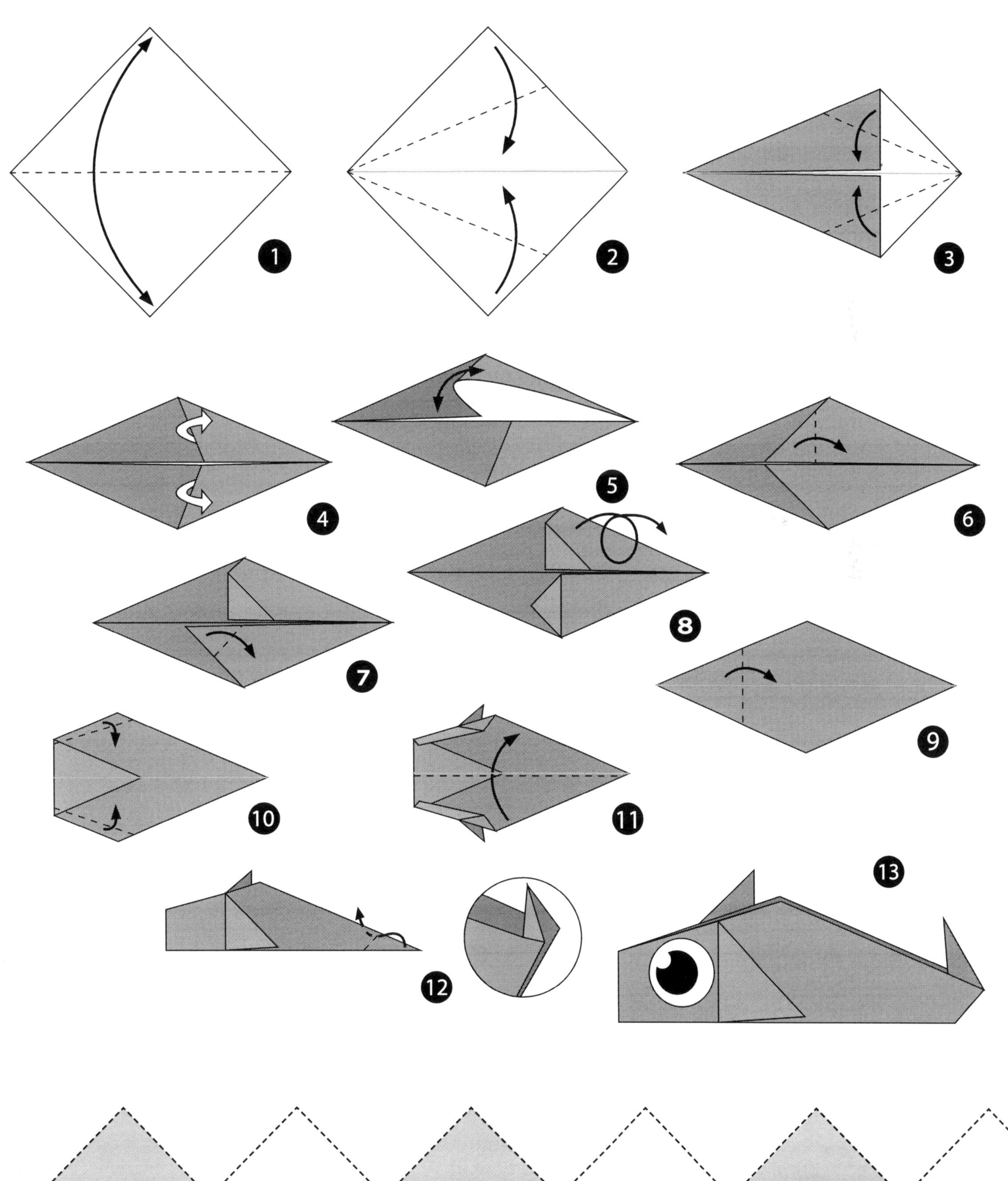

Reindeer

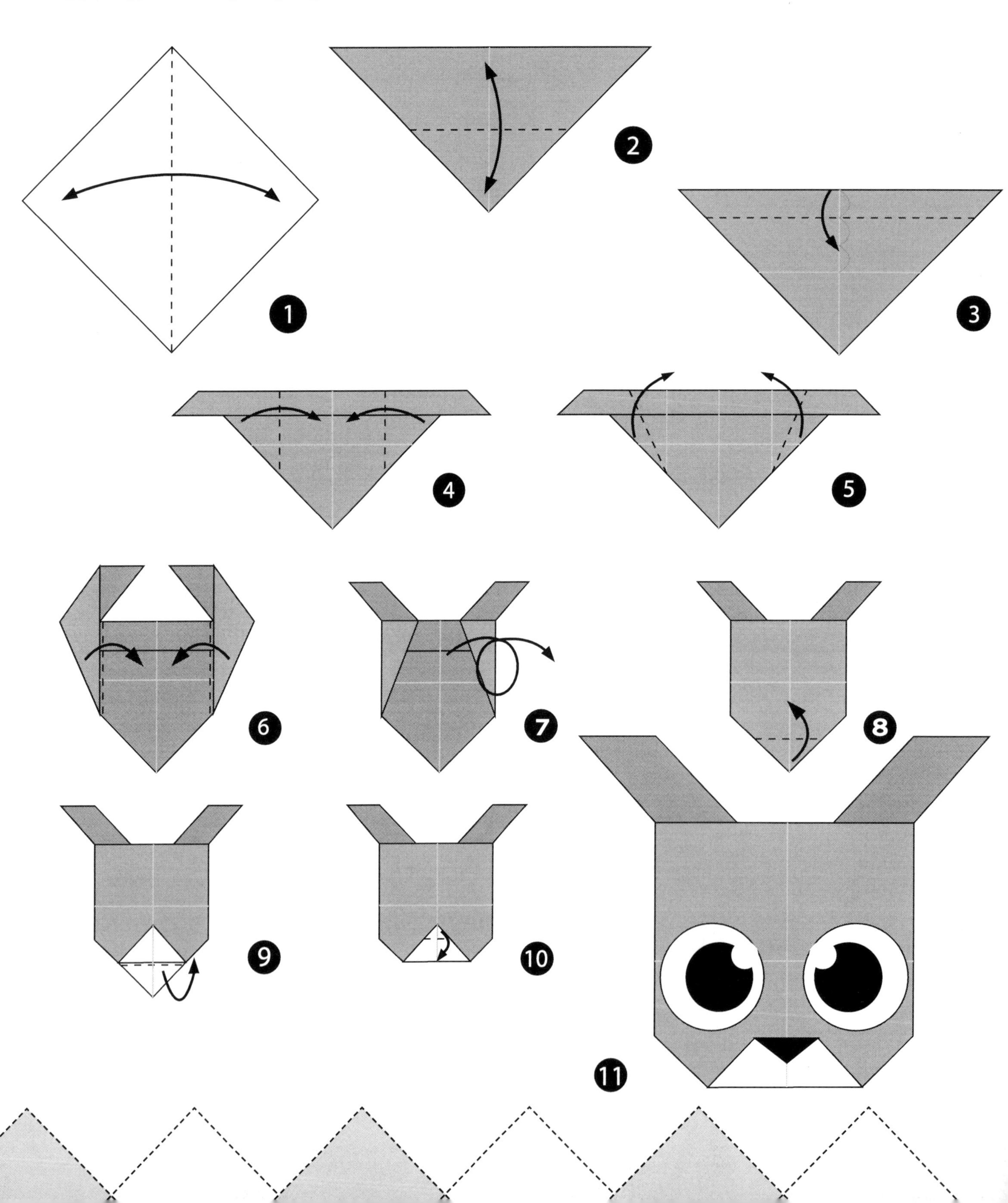

Scottie Dog

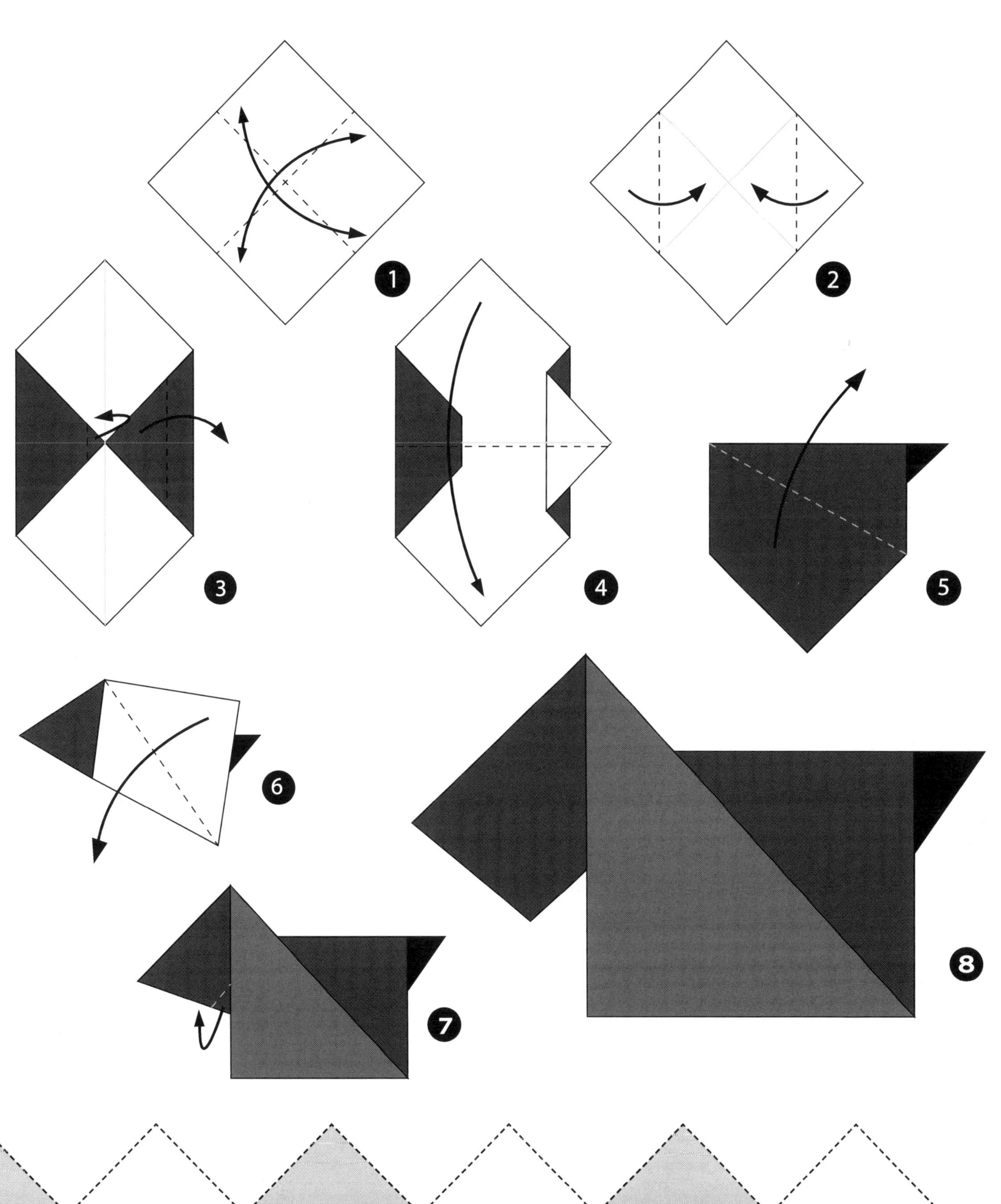

Triceratops

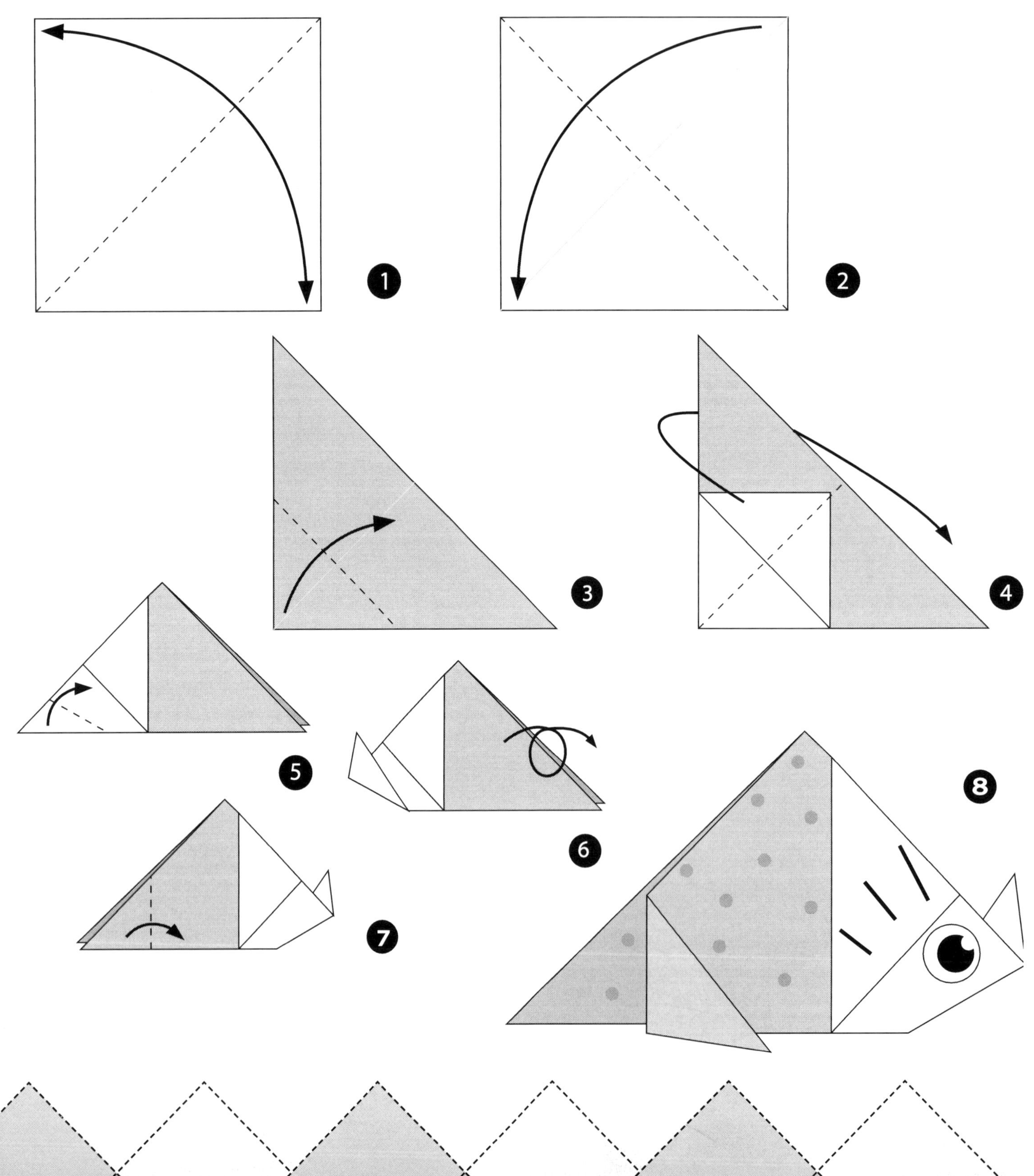

A Boy

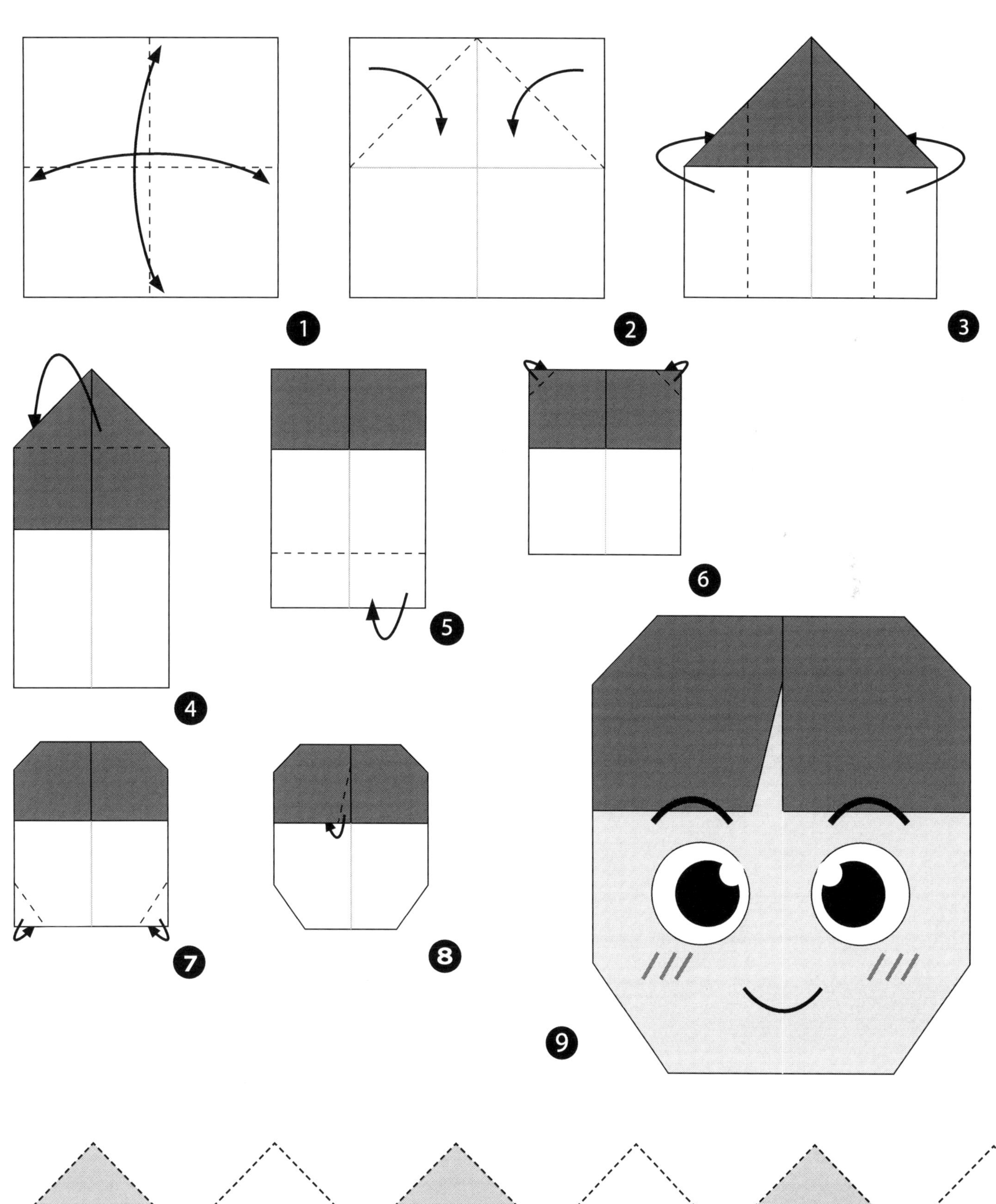

Bird

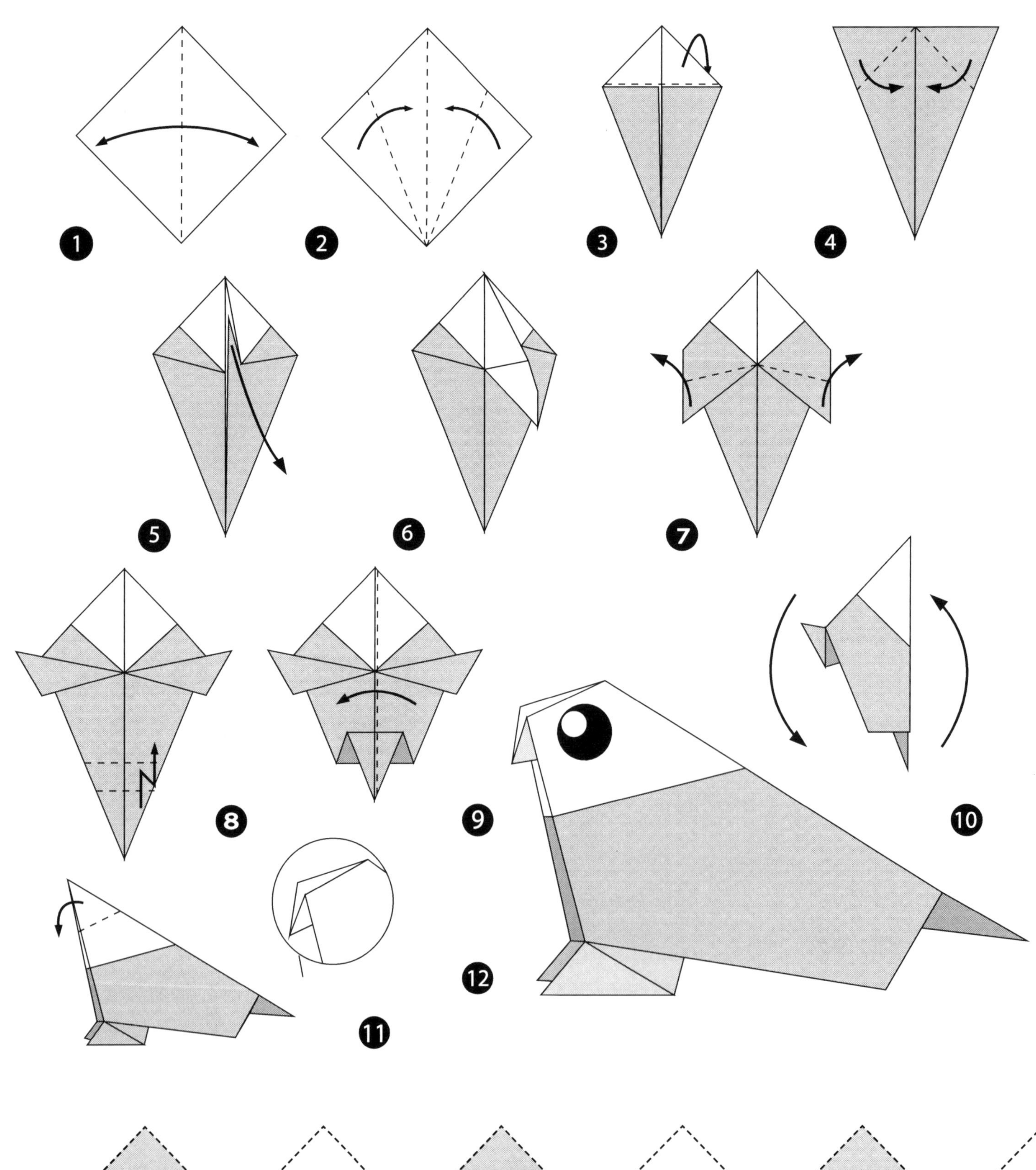

Boat

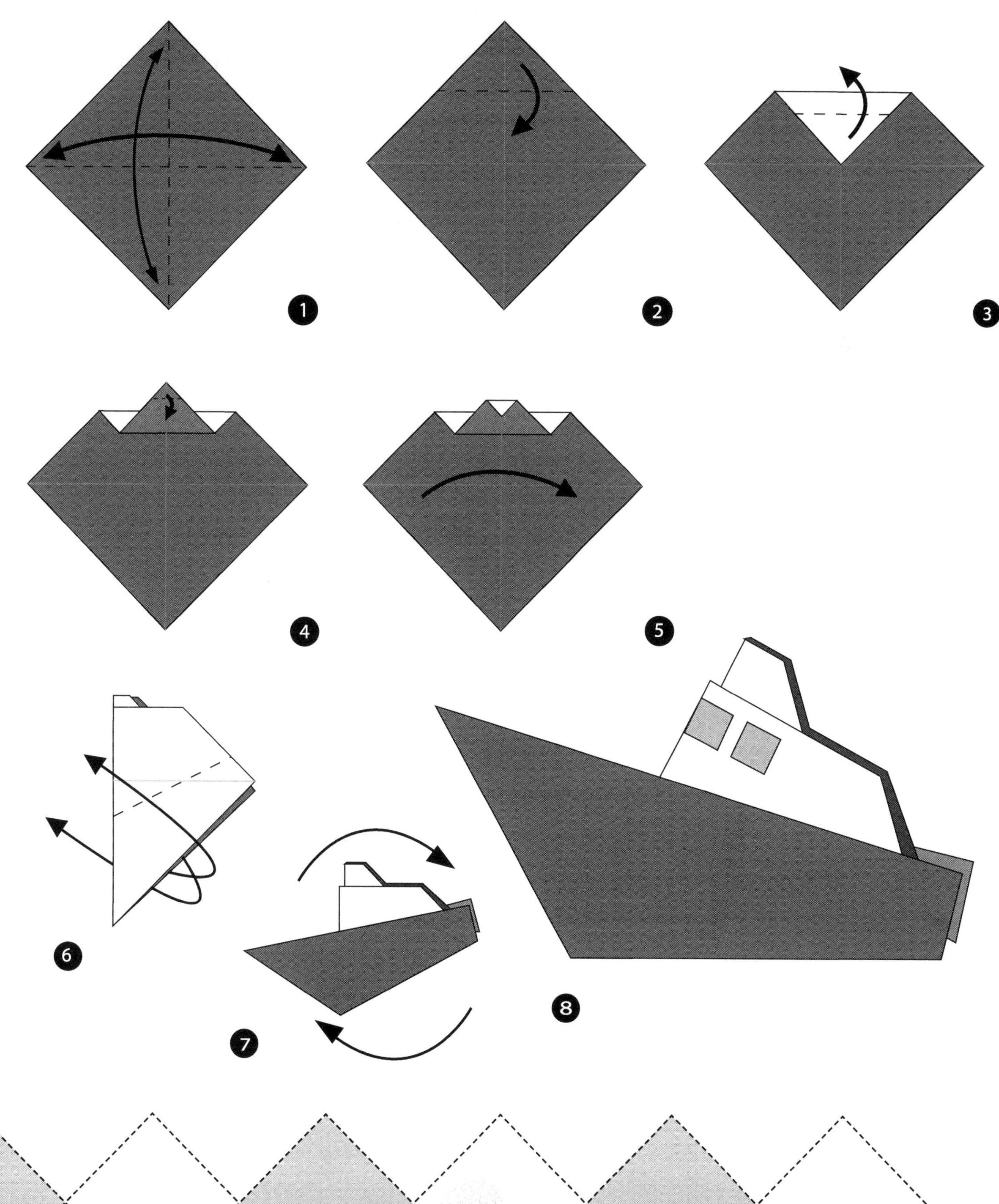

Bulldog

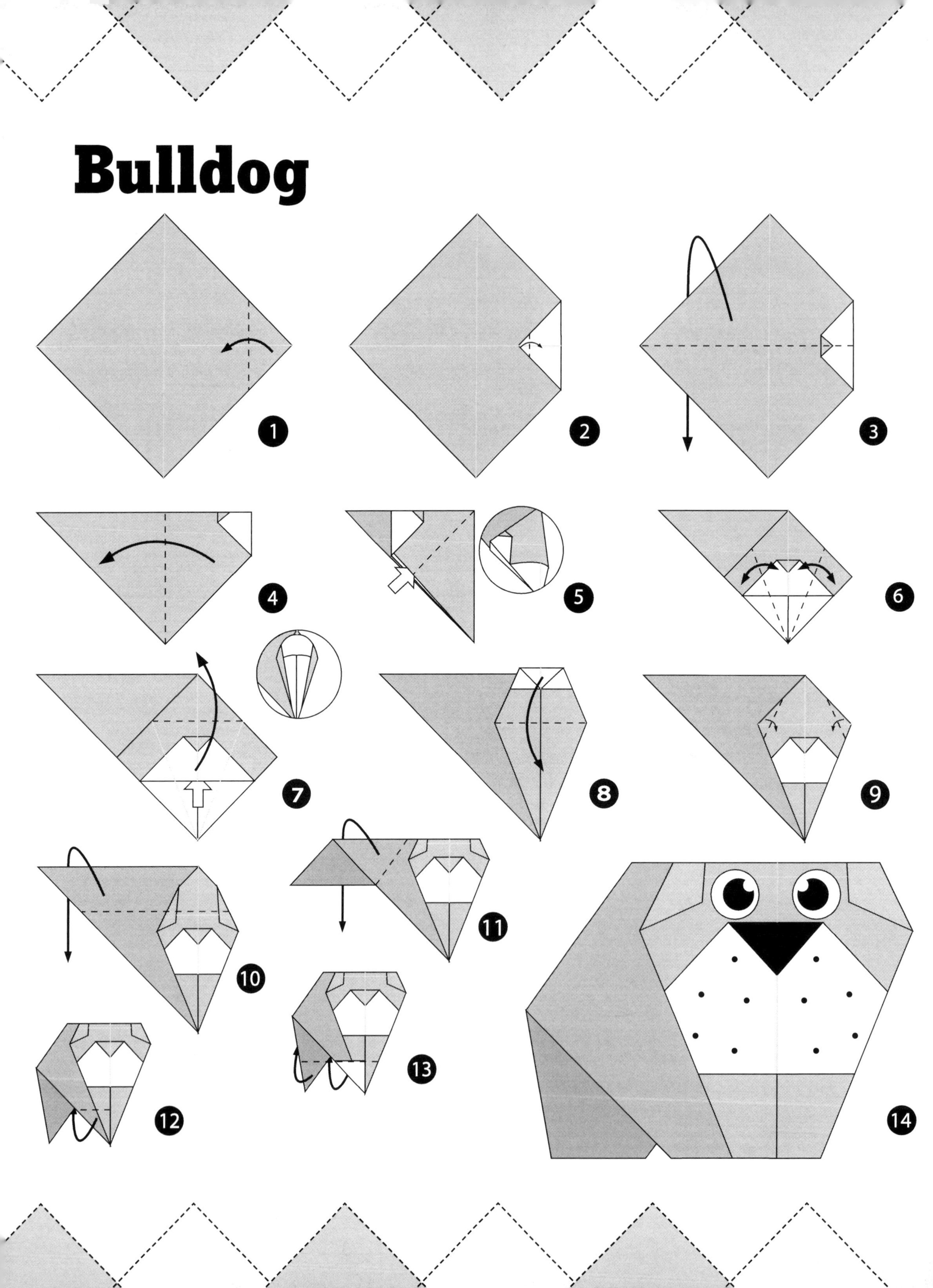

Skull

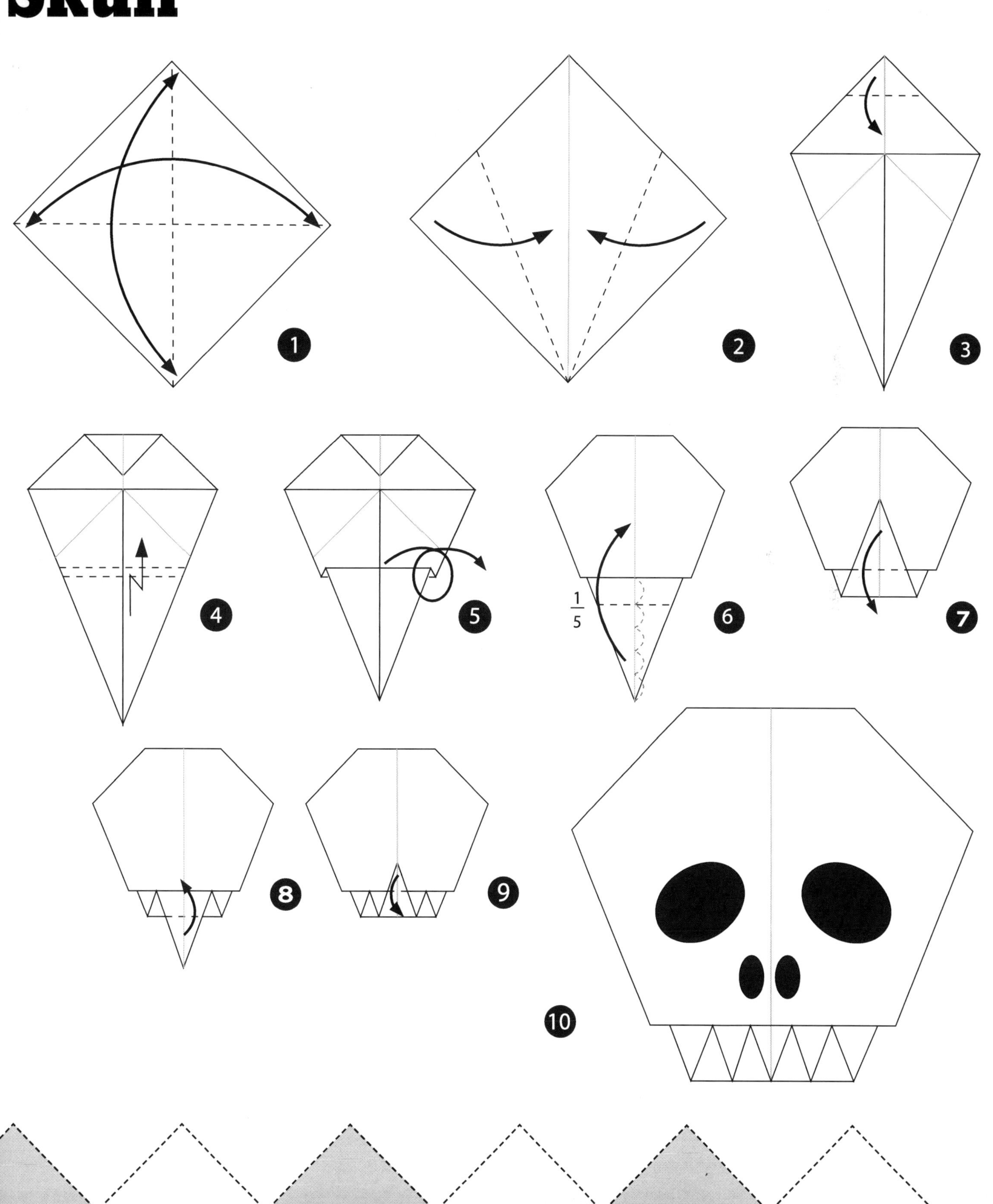

Plesiosaur

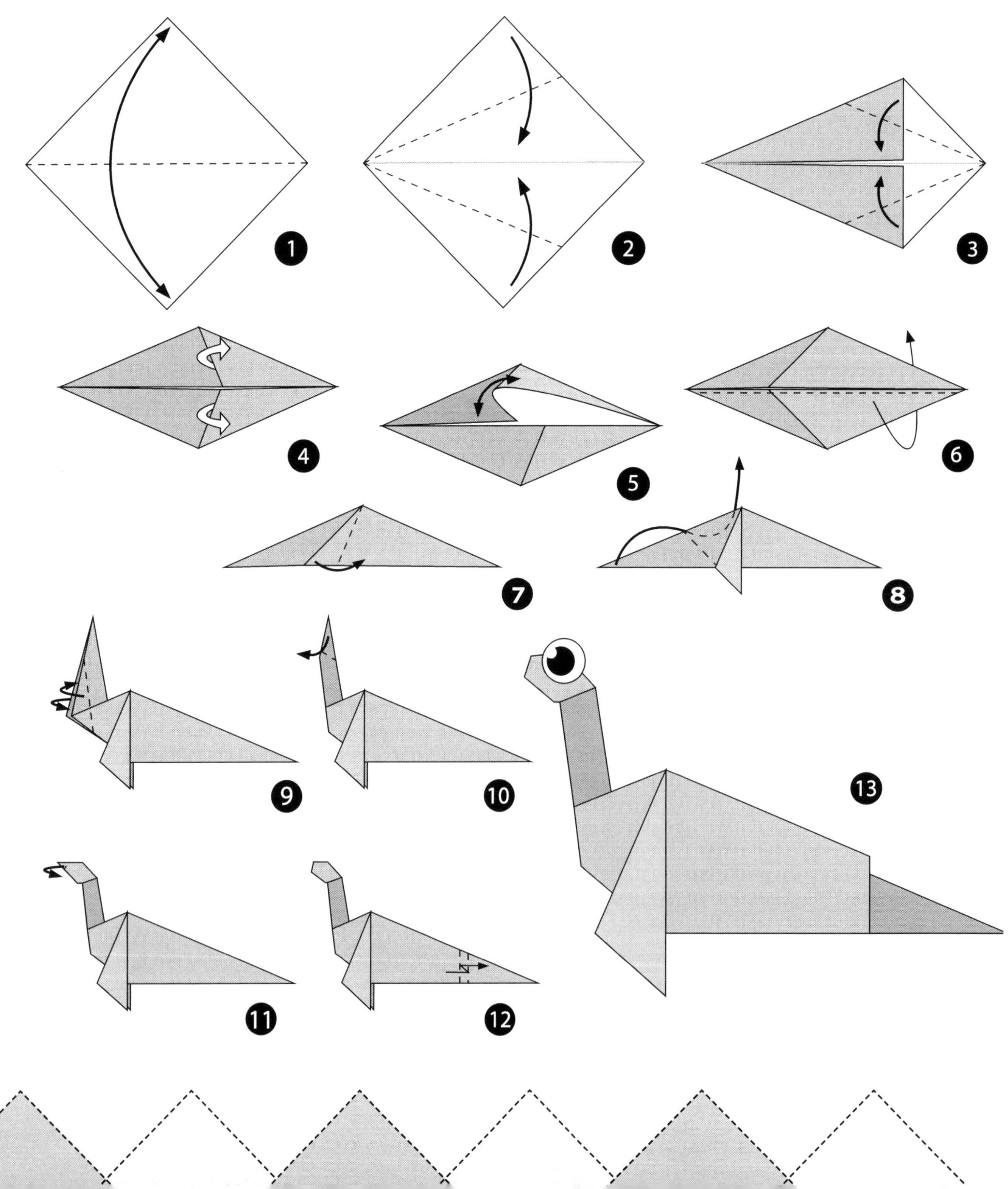

Hippo

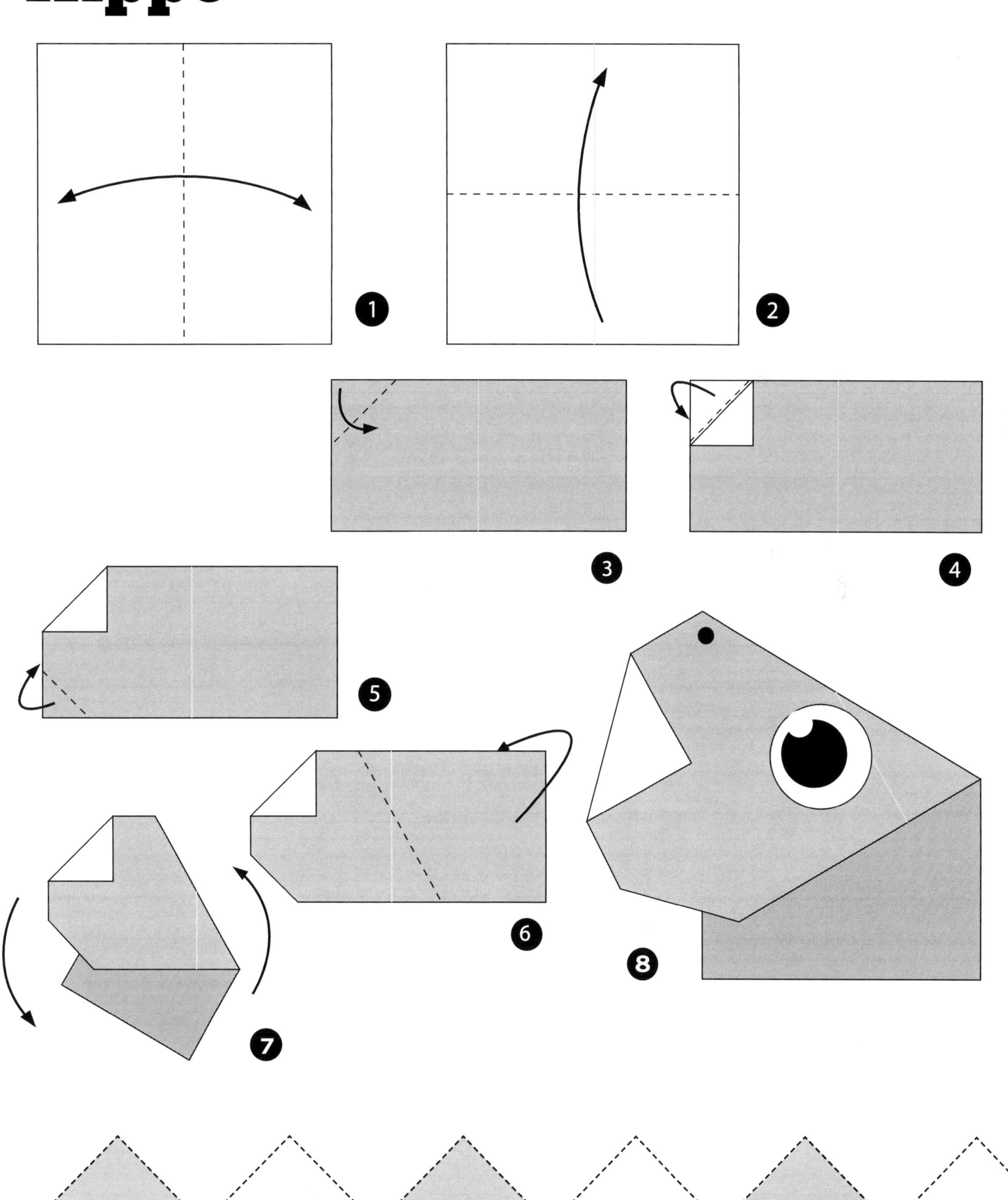

Snake

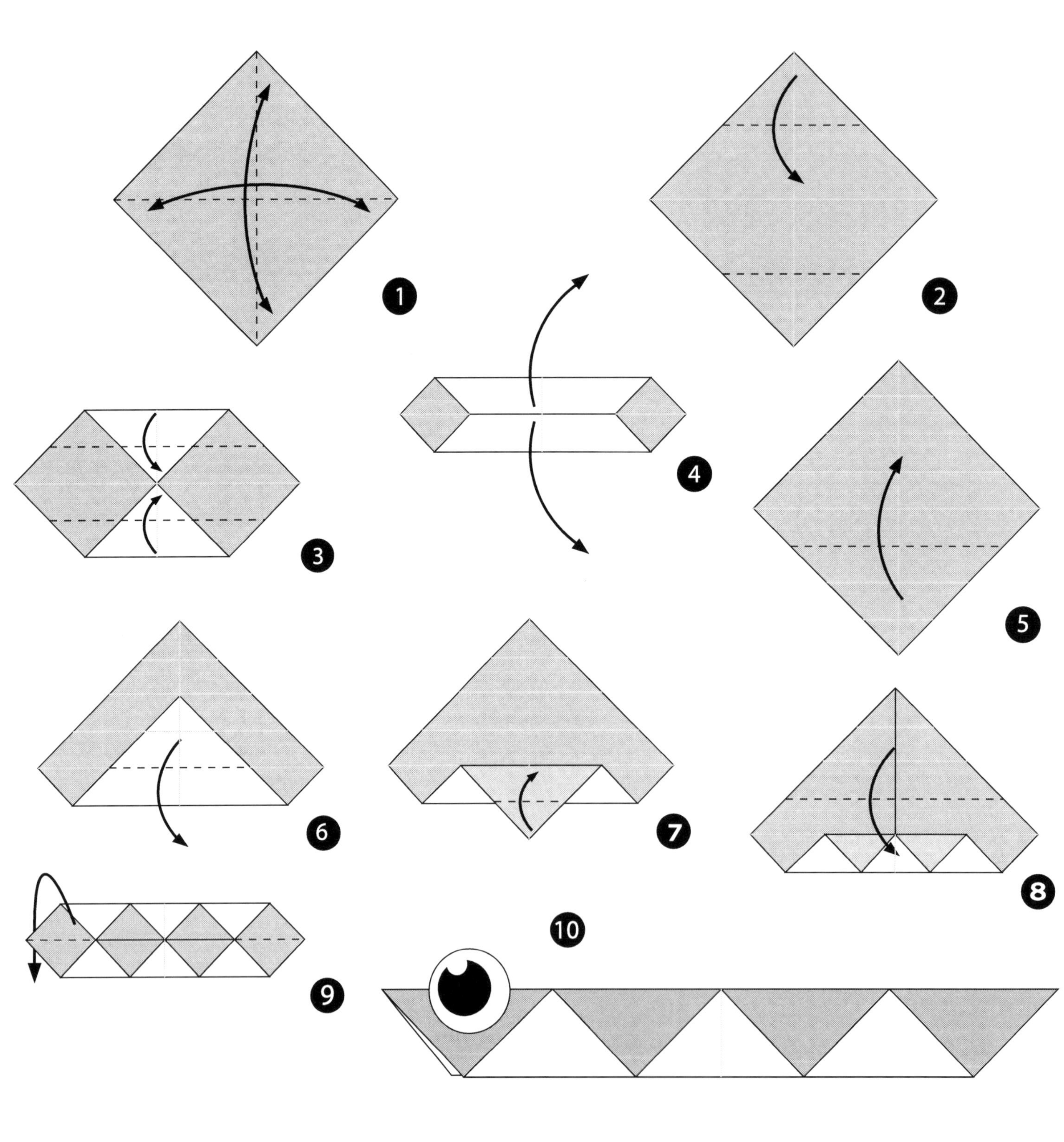

Crocodile

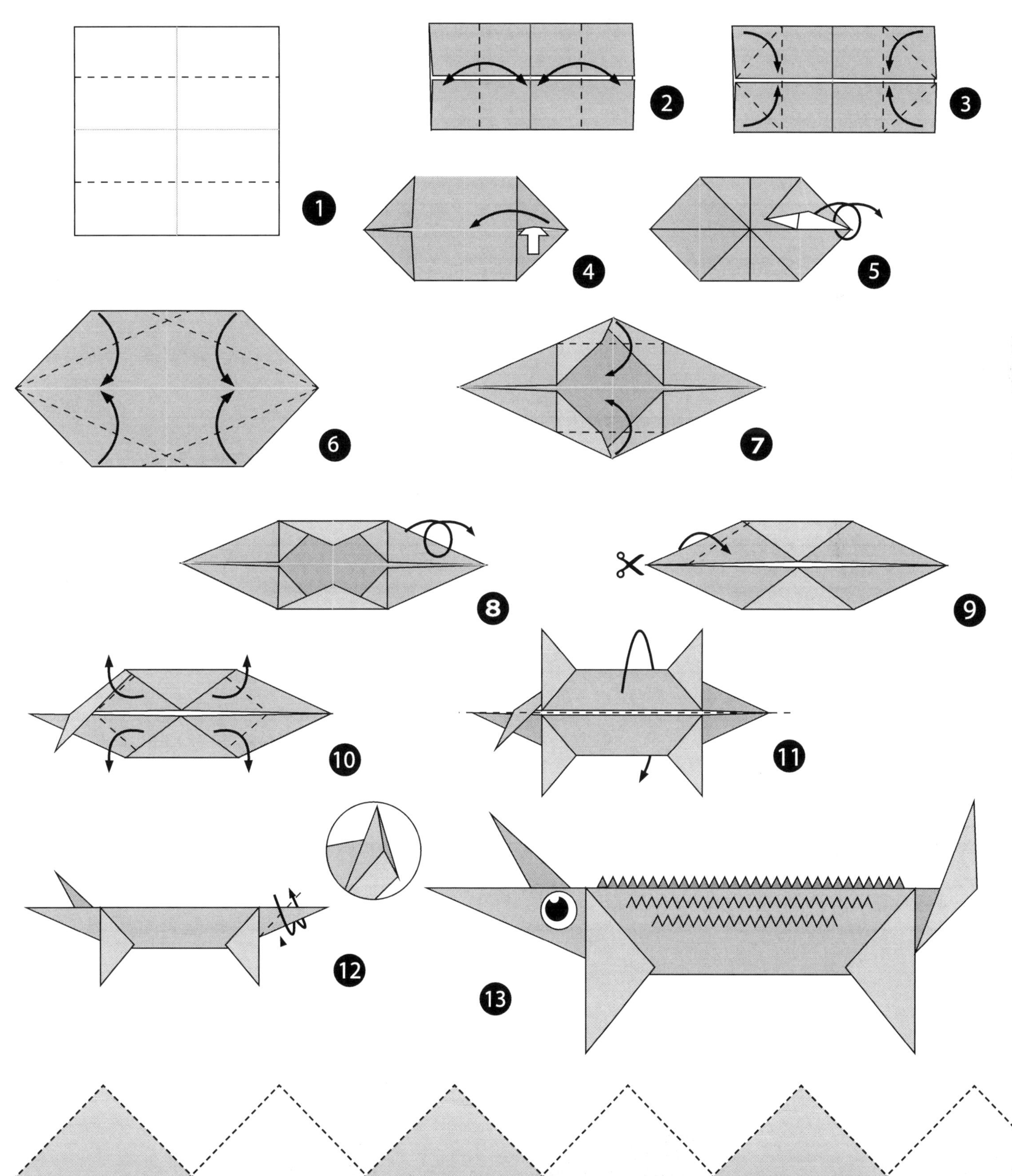

Crab

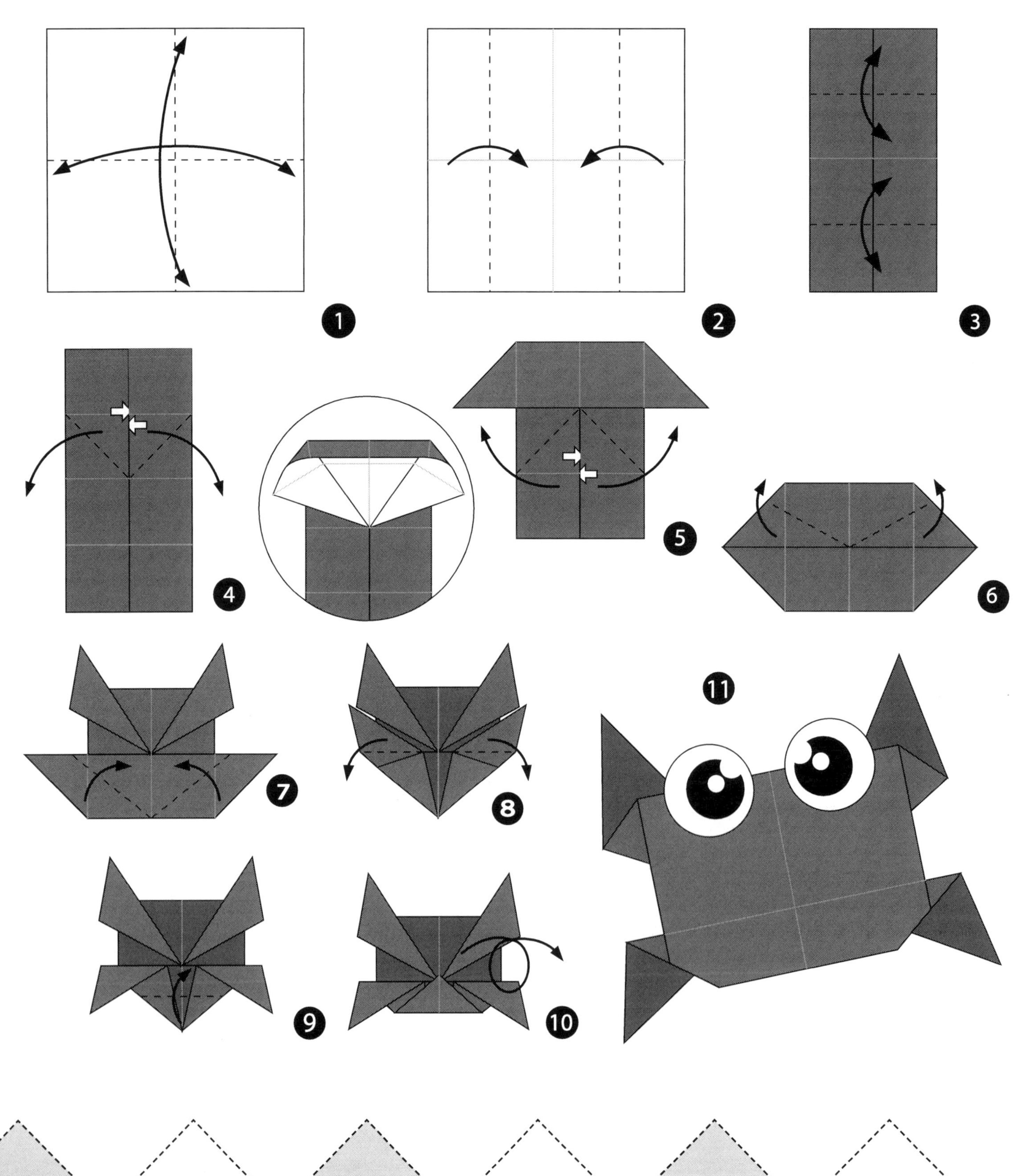

Baby Chick

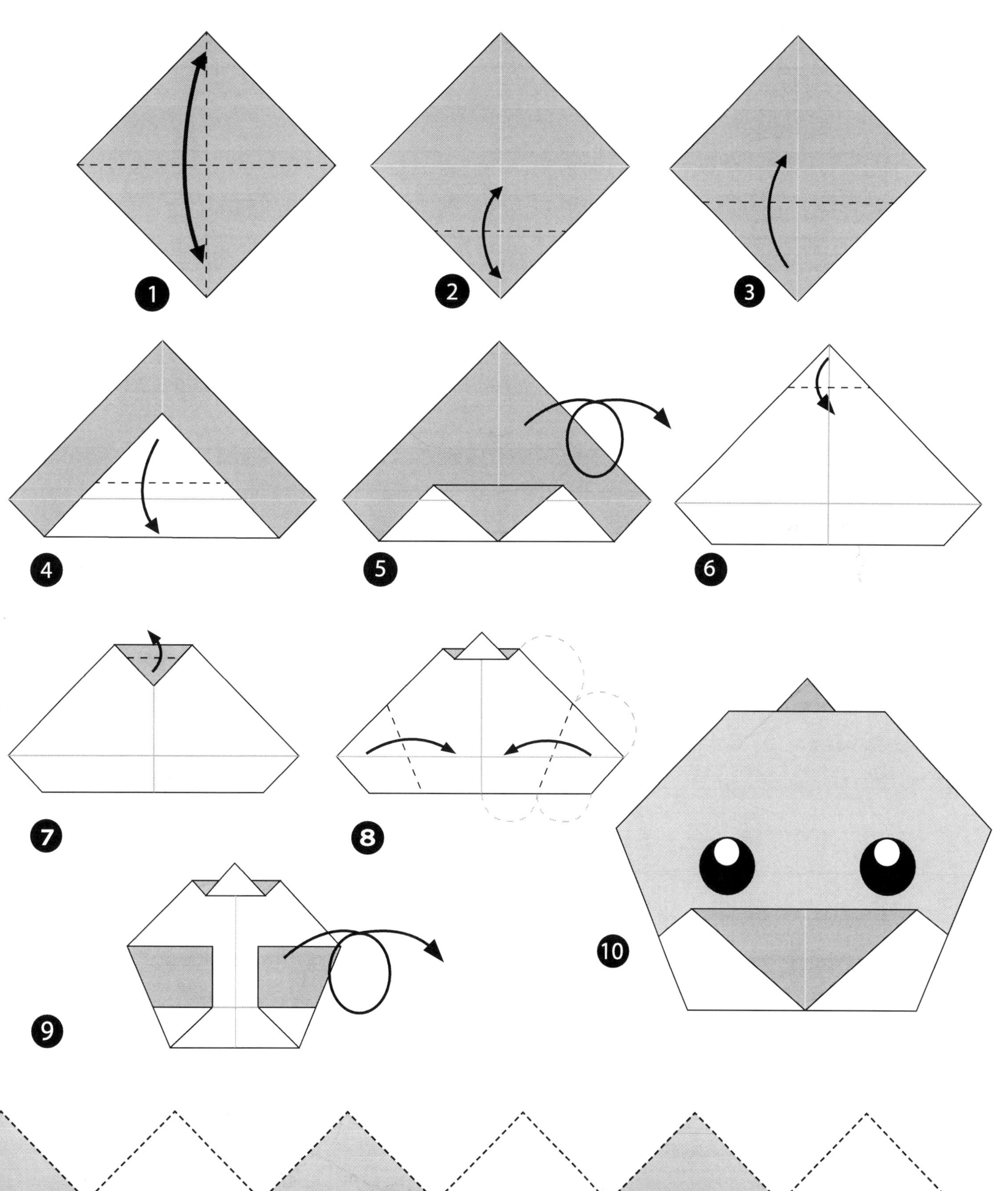

Pigeon

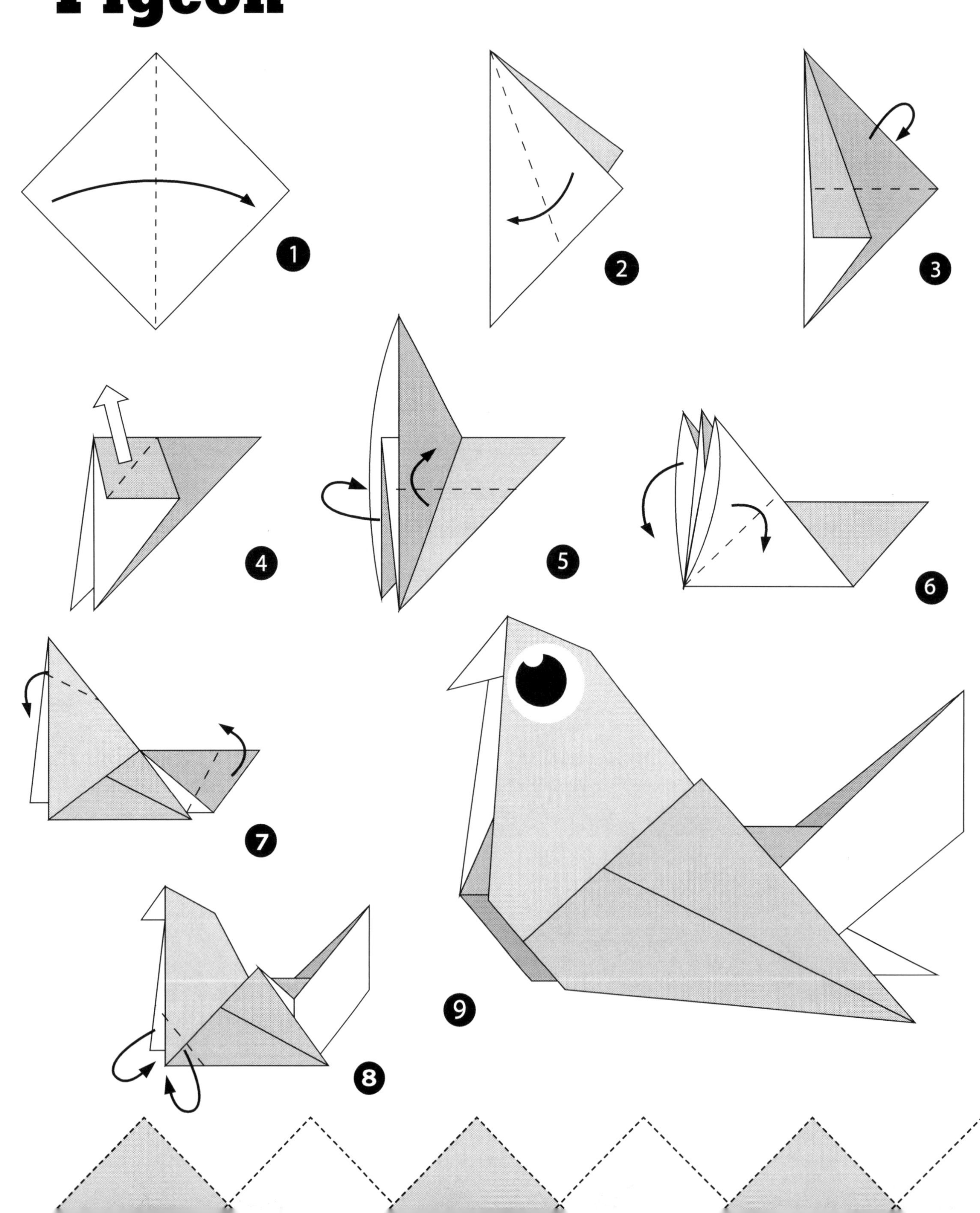

A Wallet

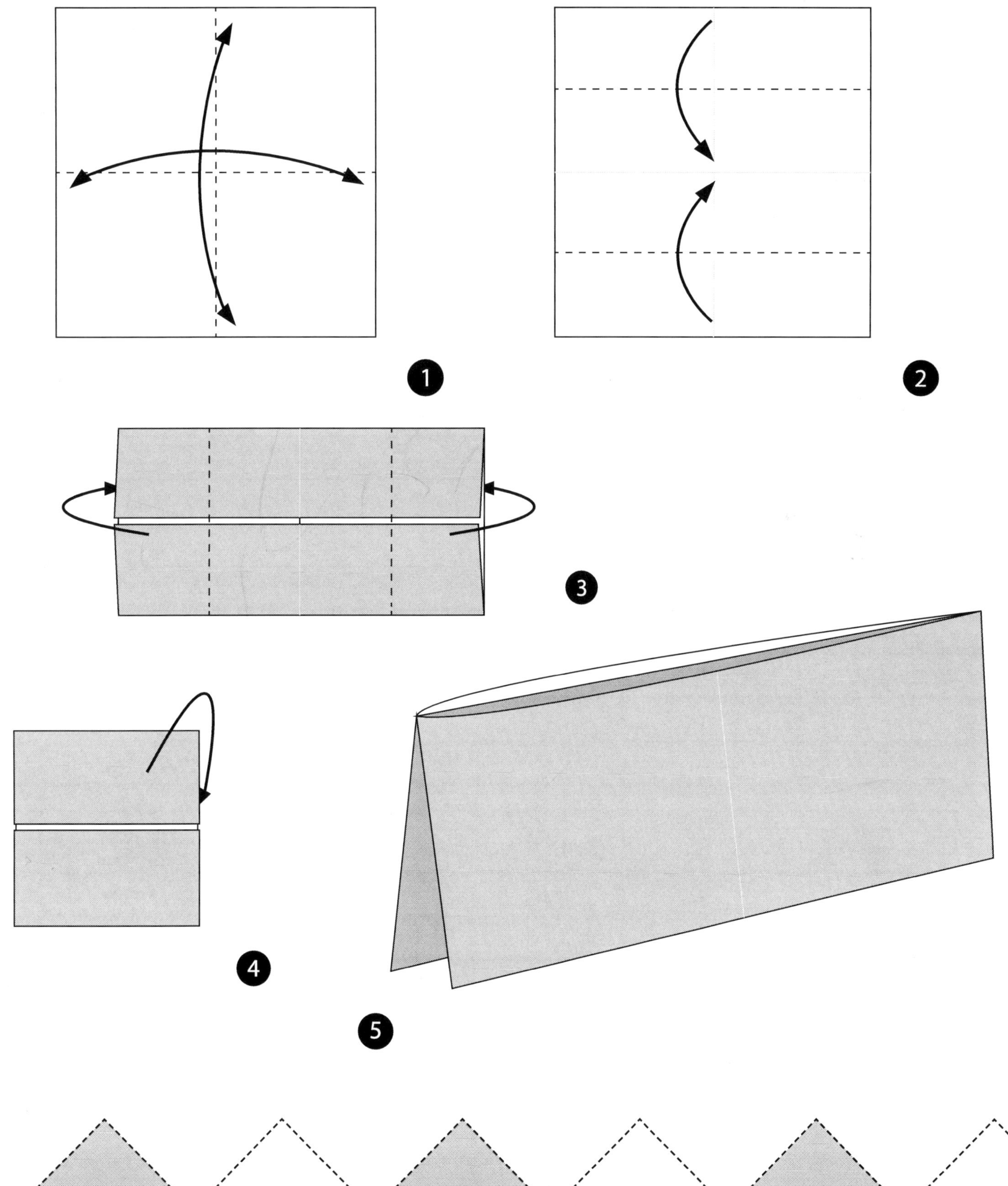

Cow

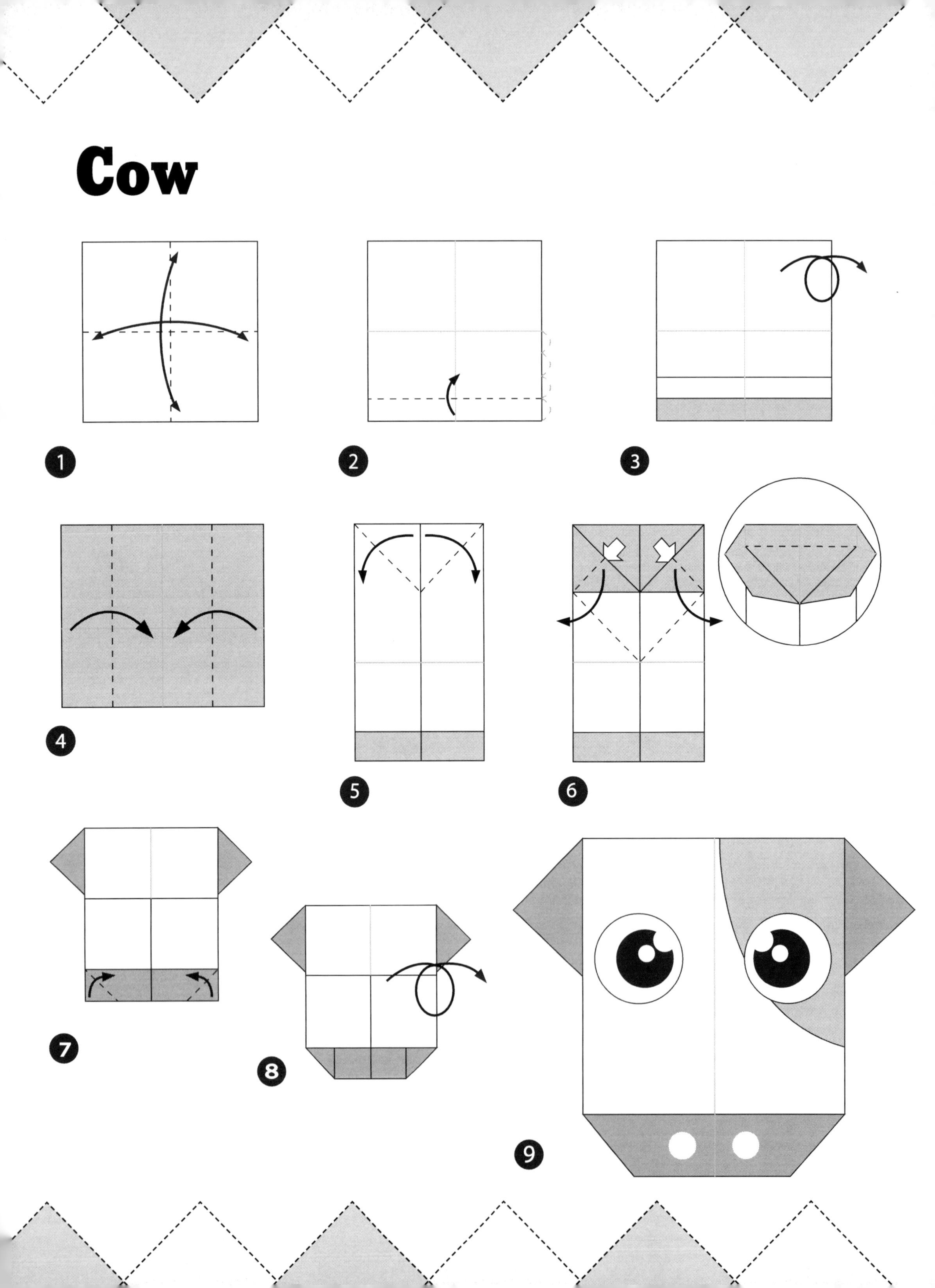

Dracula

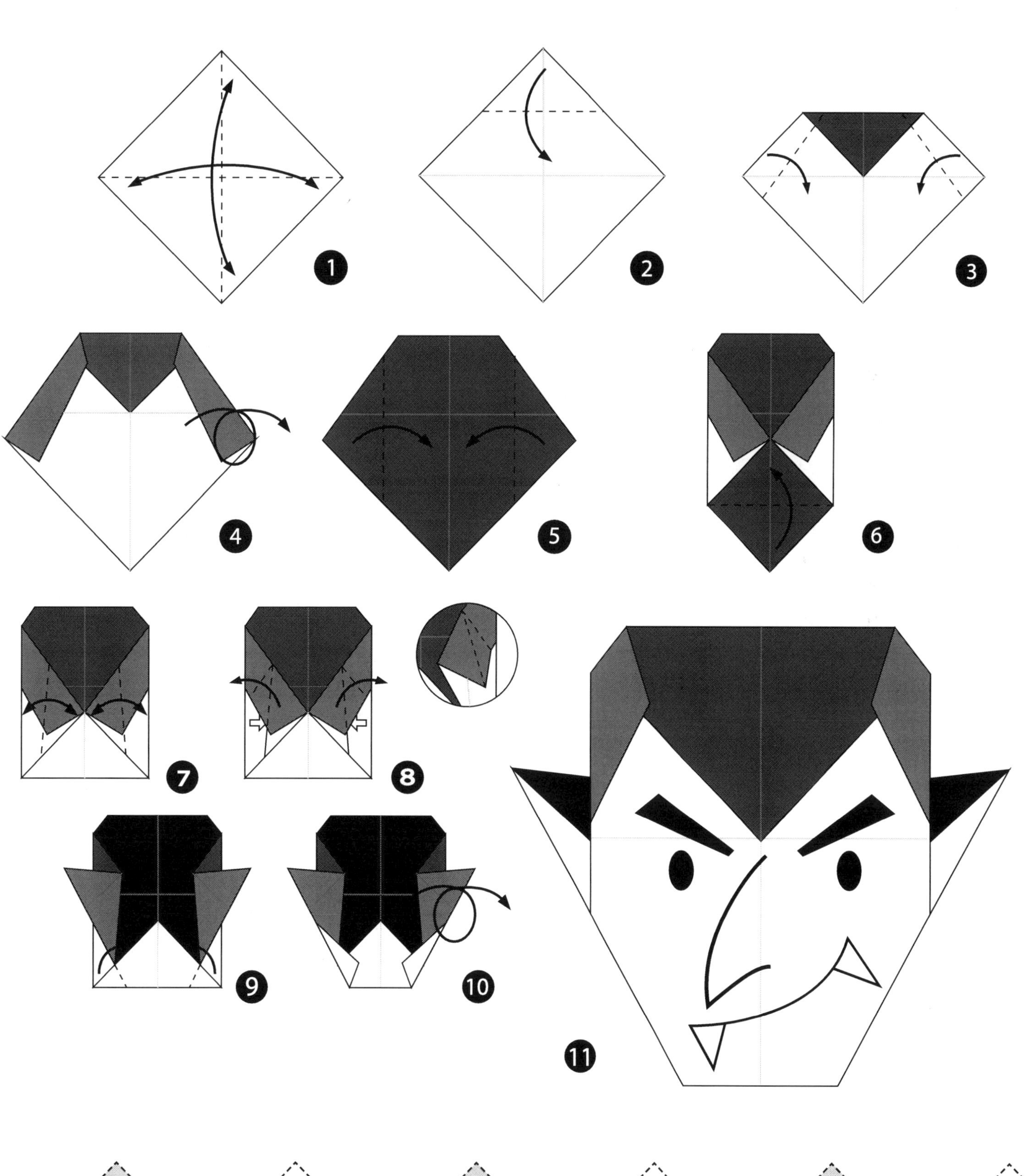

UFO

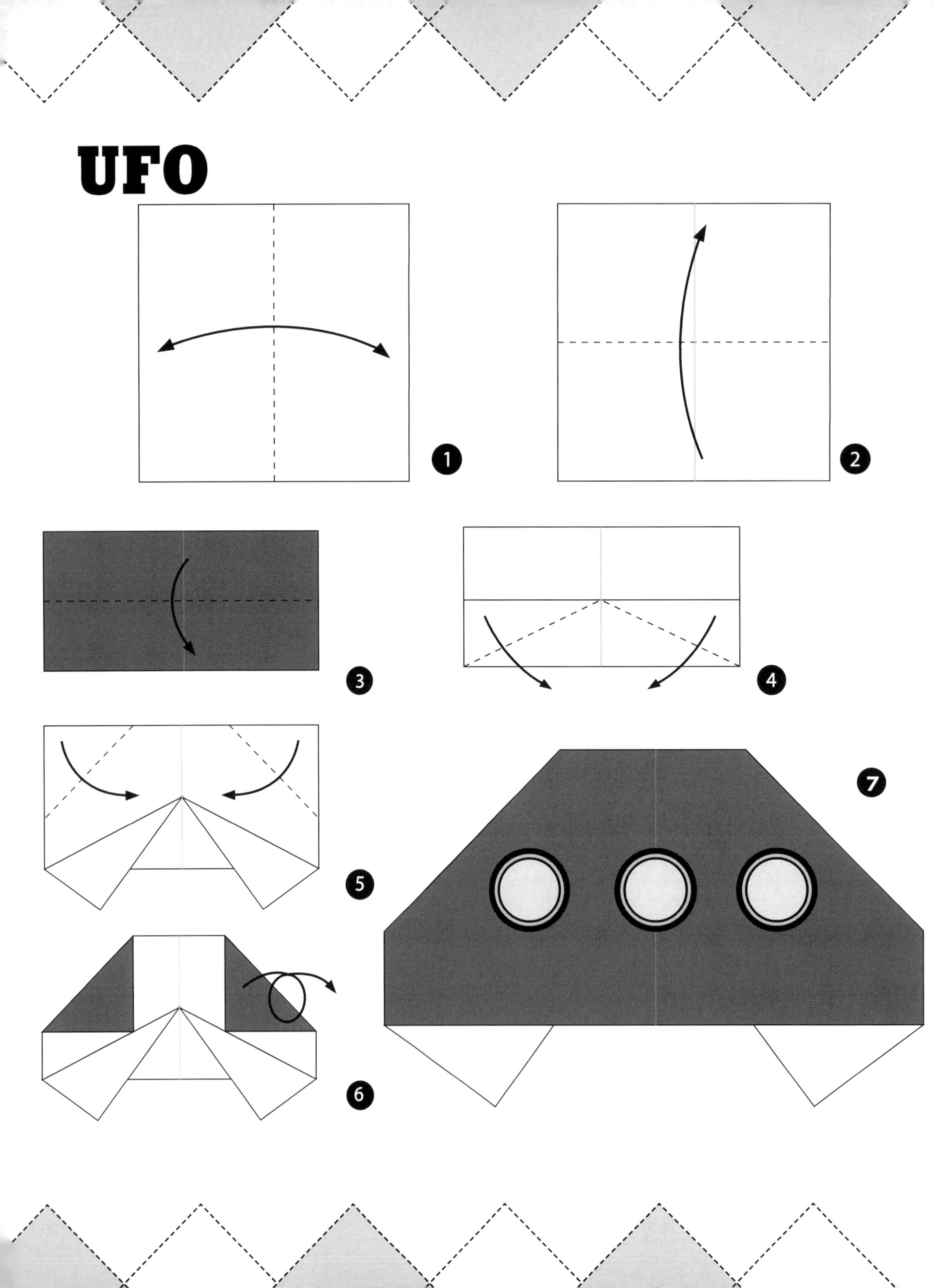

Pig

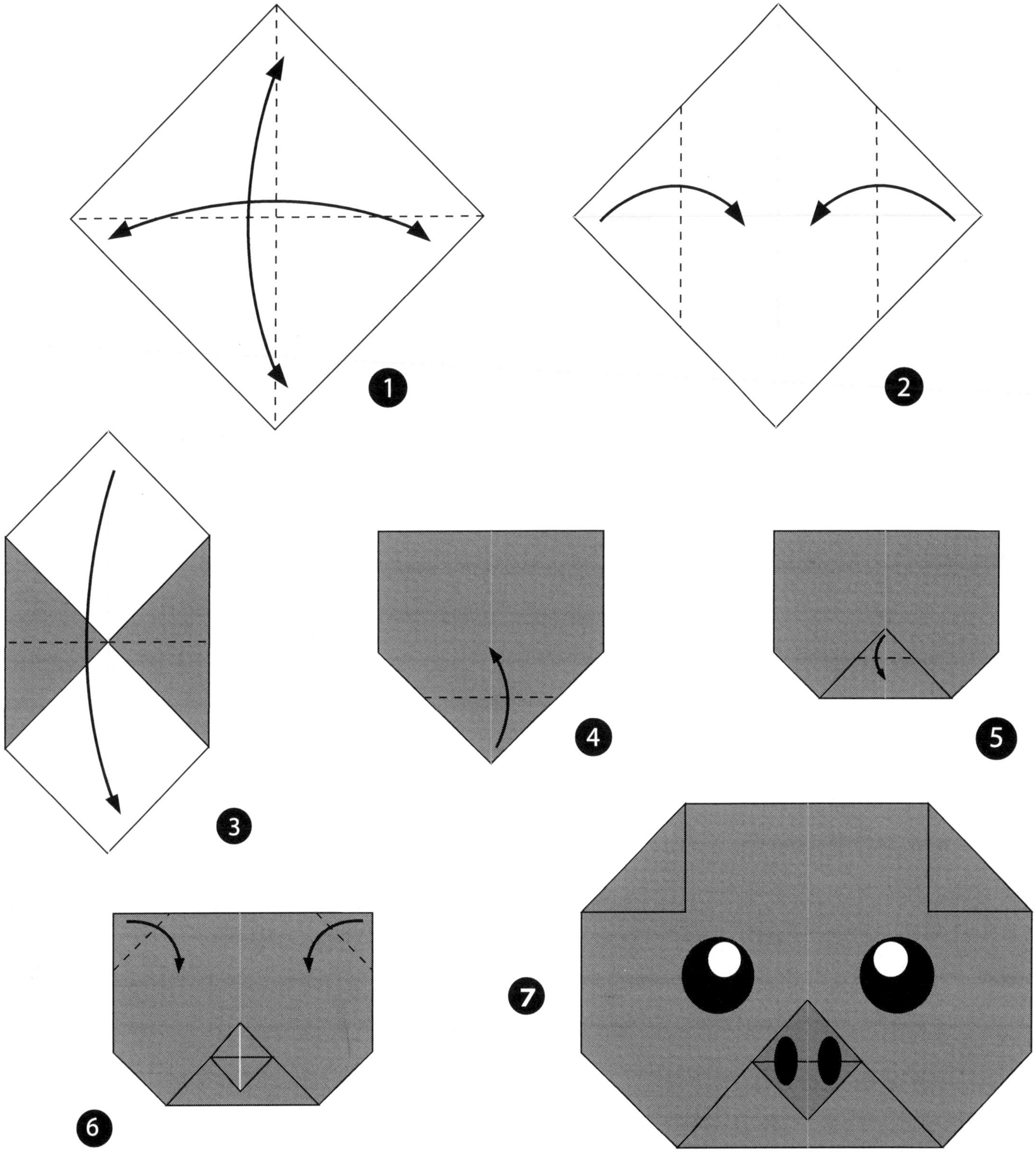

1

2

3

4

5

6

7

Poodle

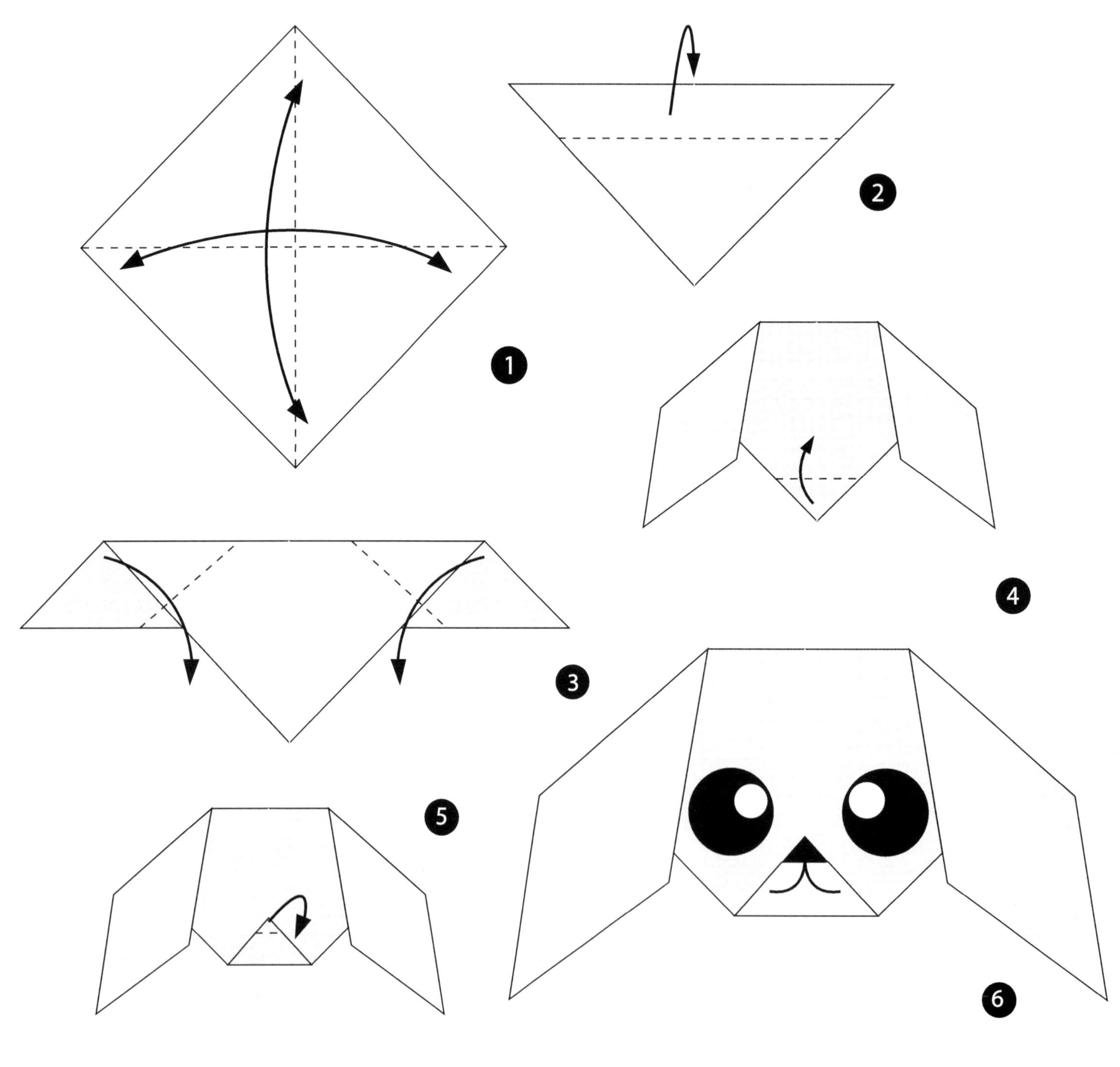

Owl

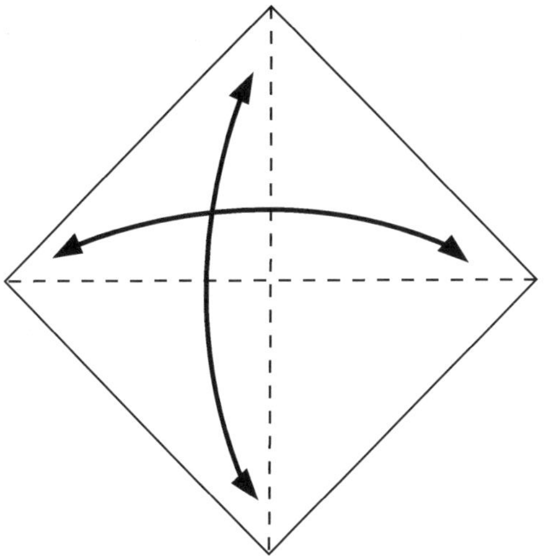

1/3

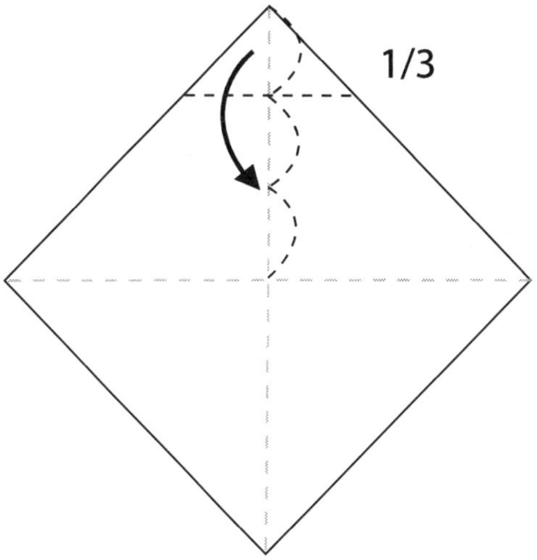

1

2

1/2

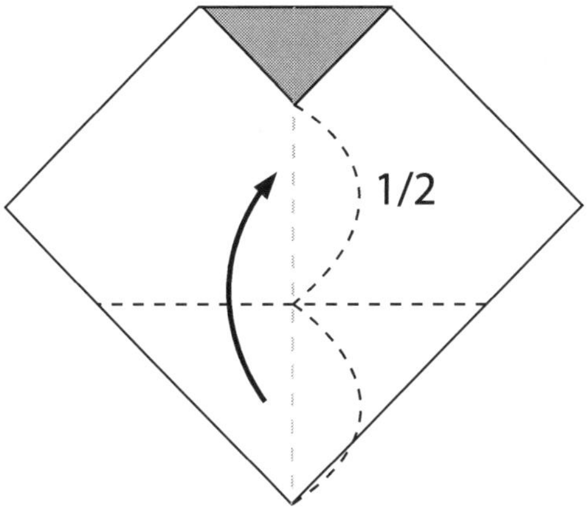

3

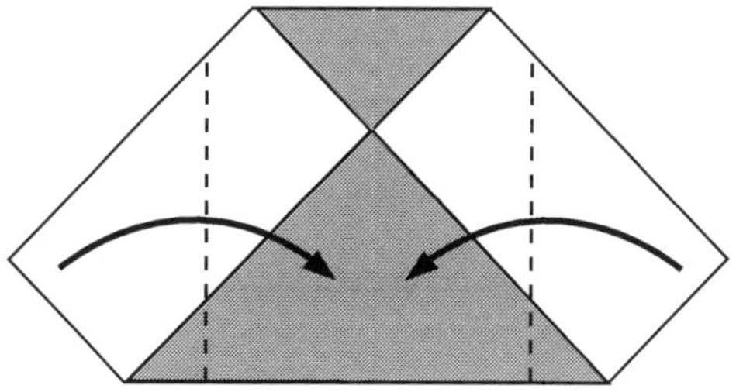

4

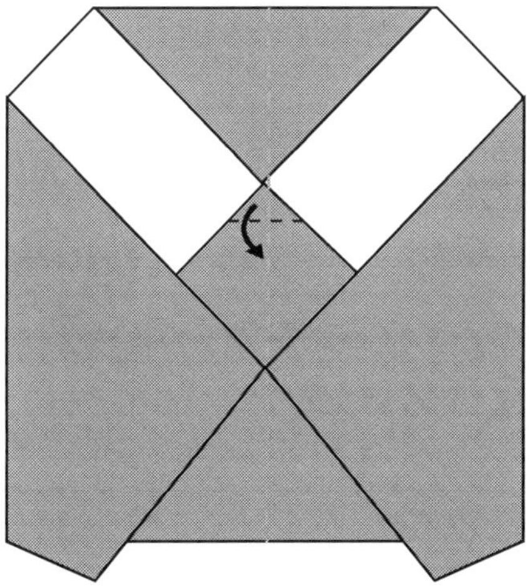

5

6

Goldfish

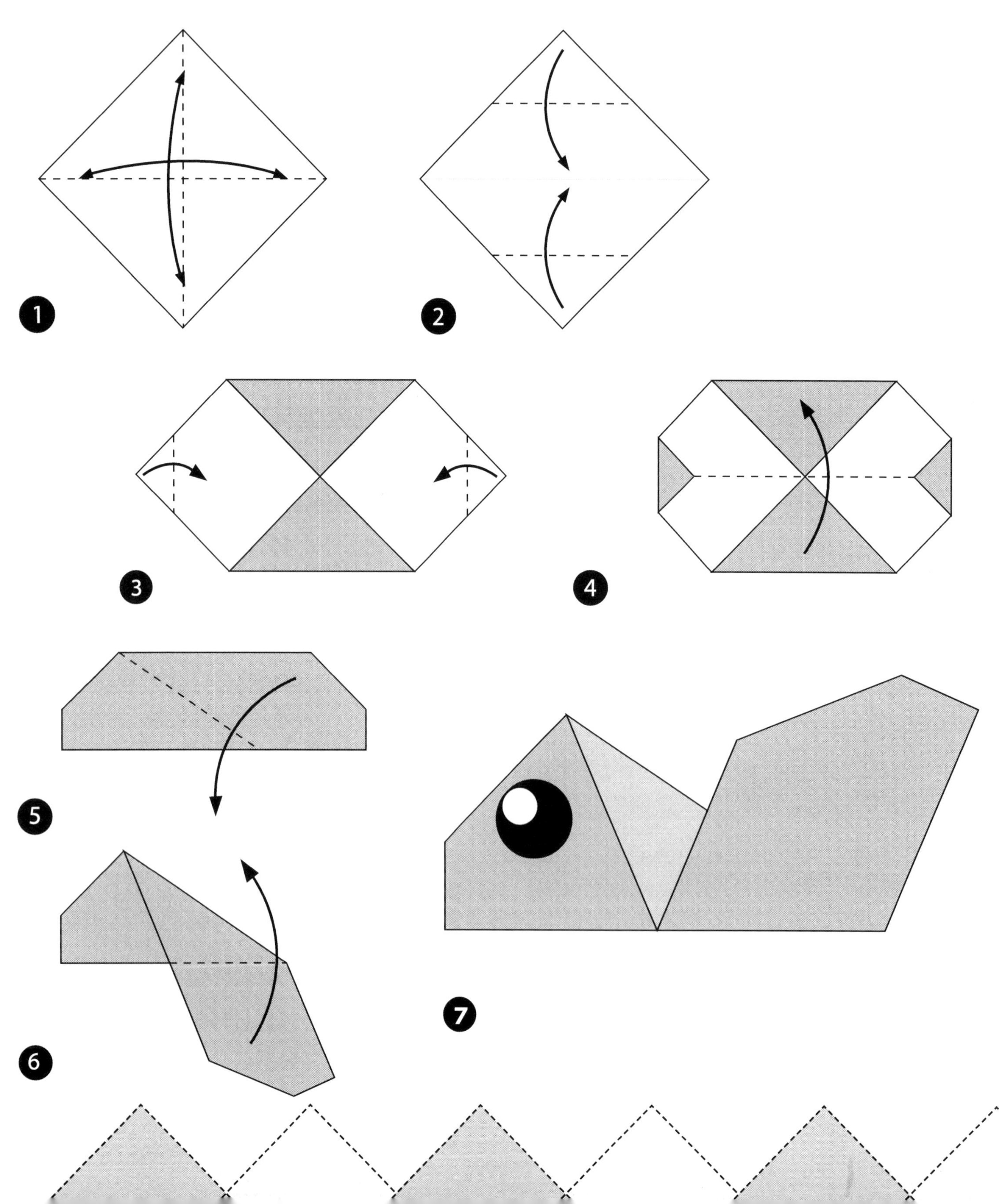

Pomeranian

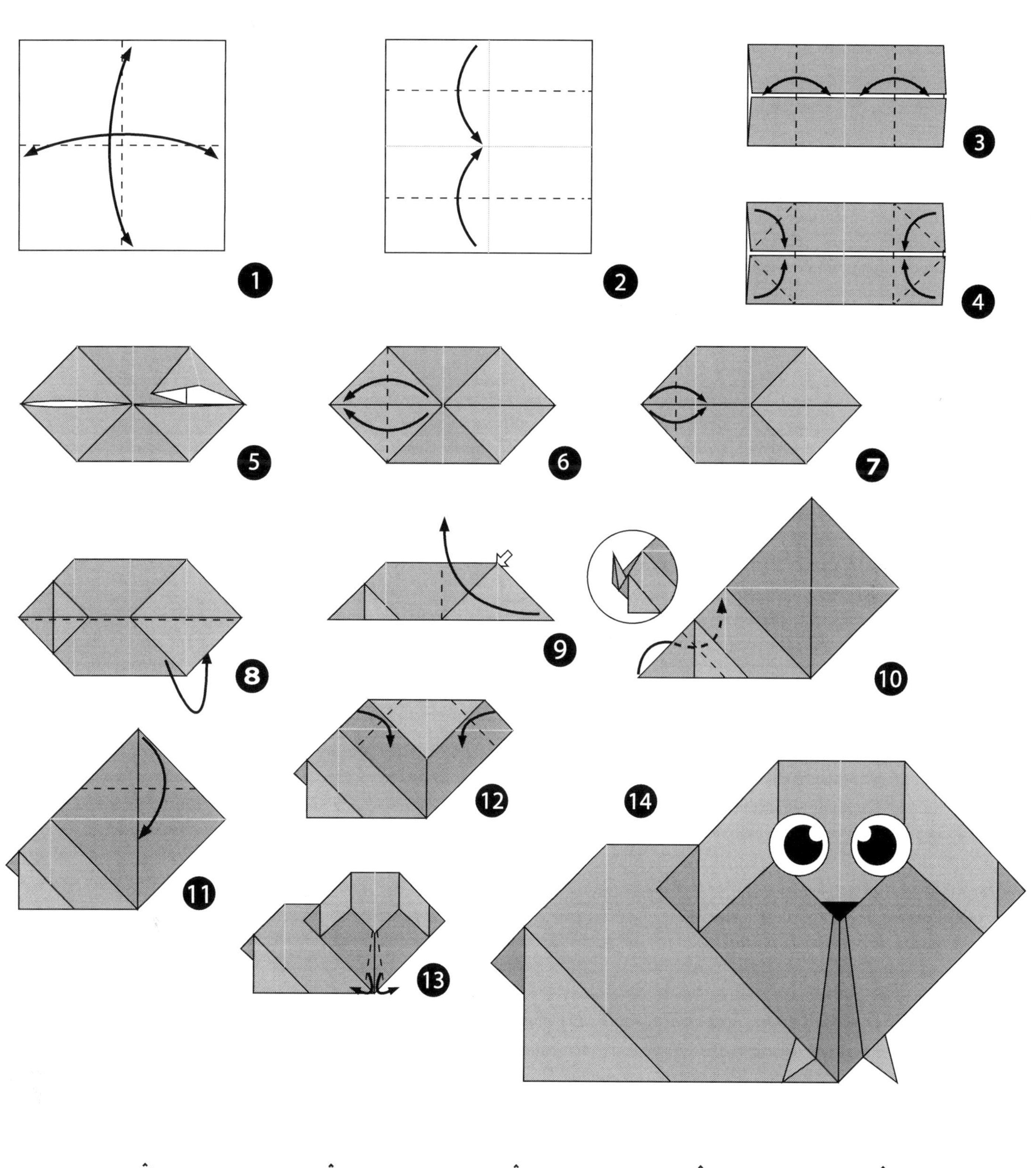

Cat

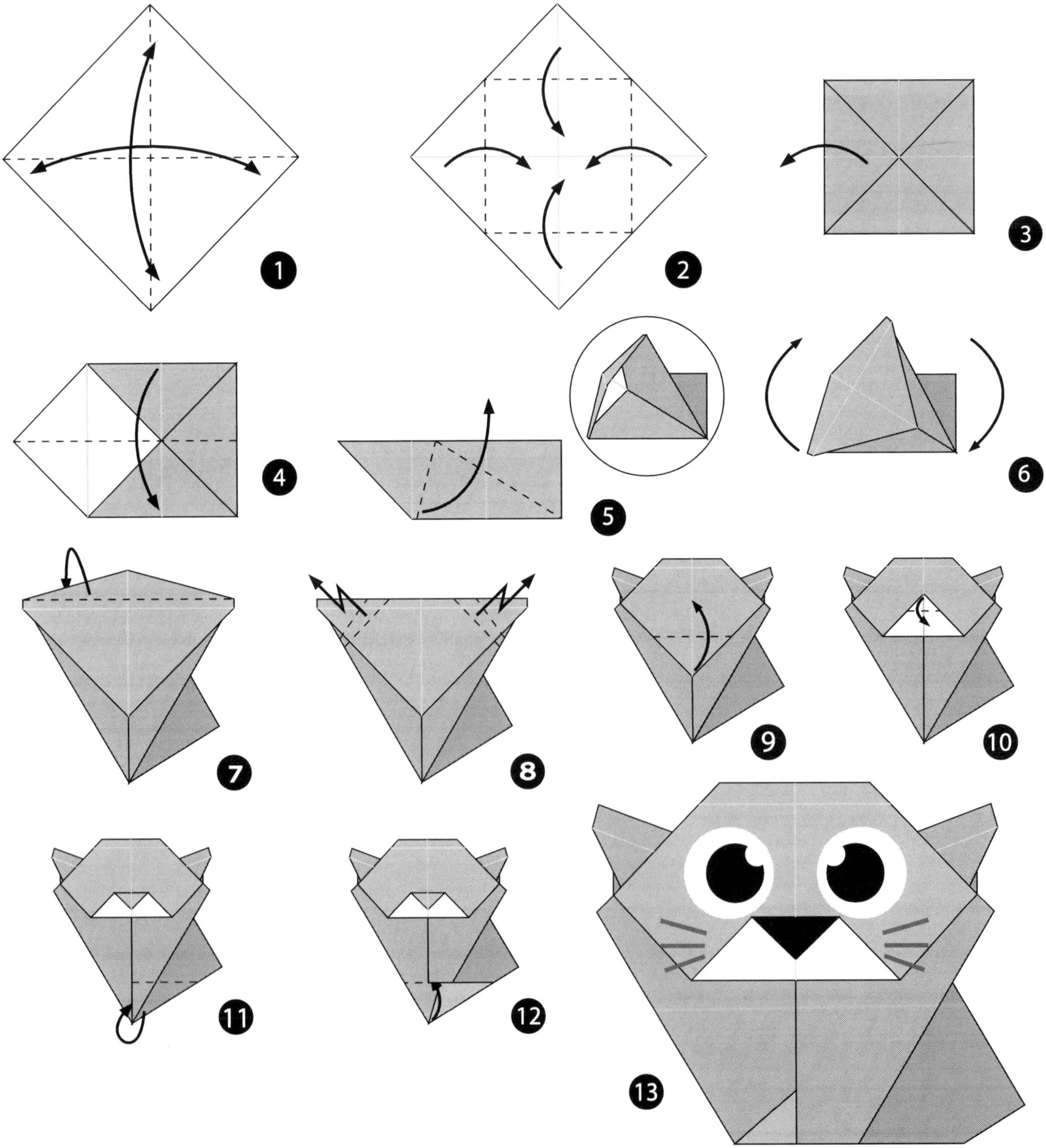

1

2

3

4

5

6

7

8

9

10

11

12

13

Bunny Box

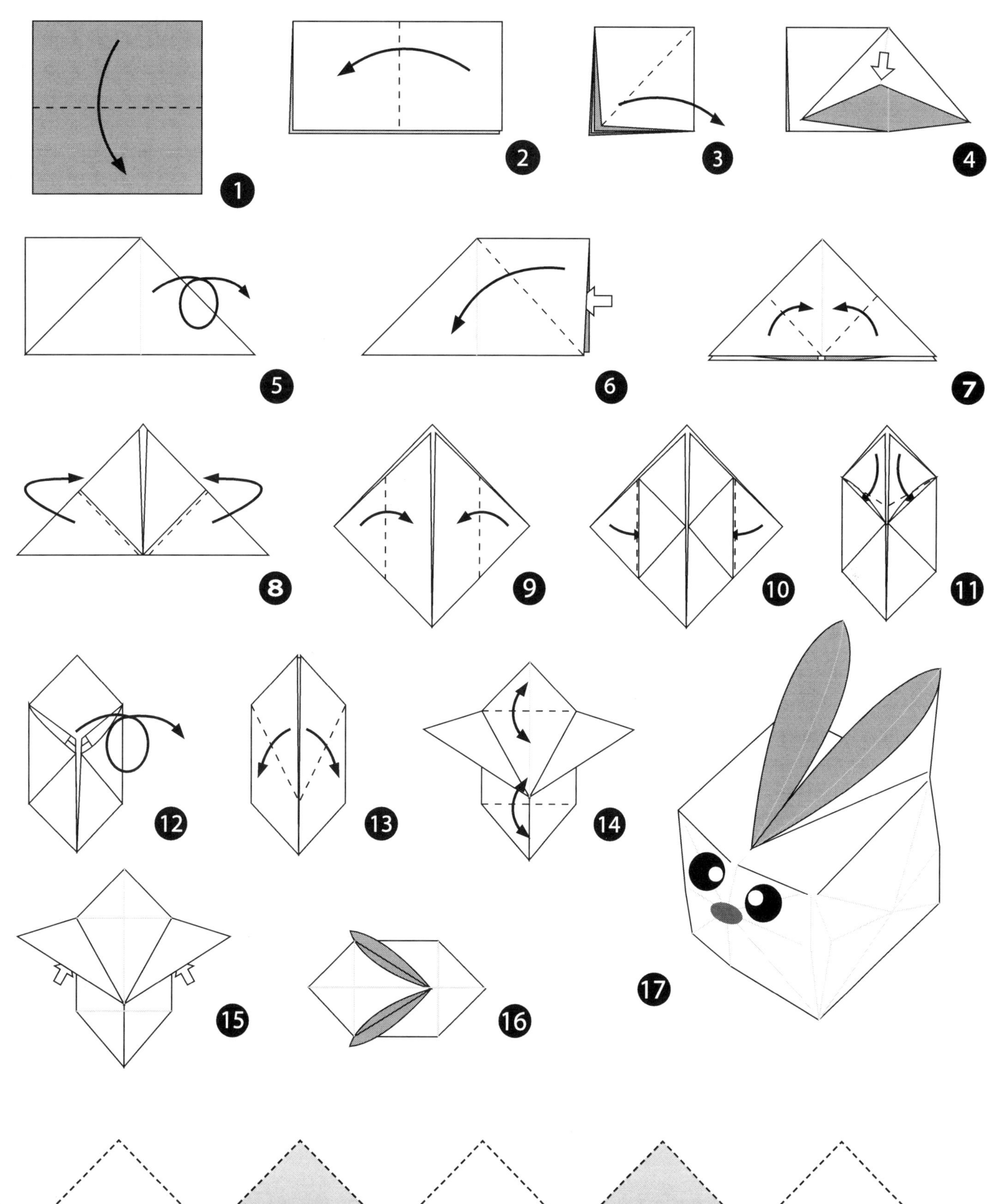

Tiger

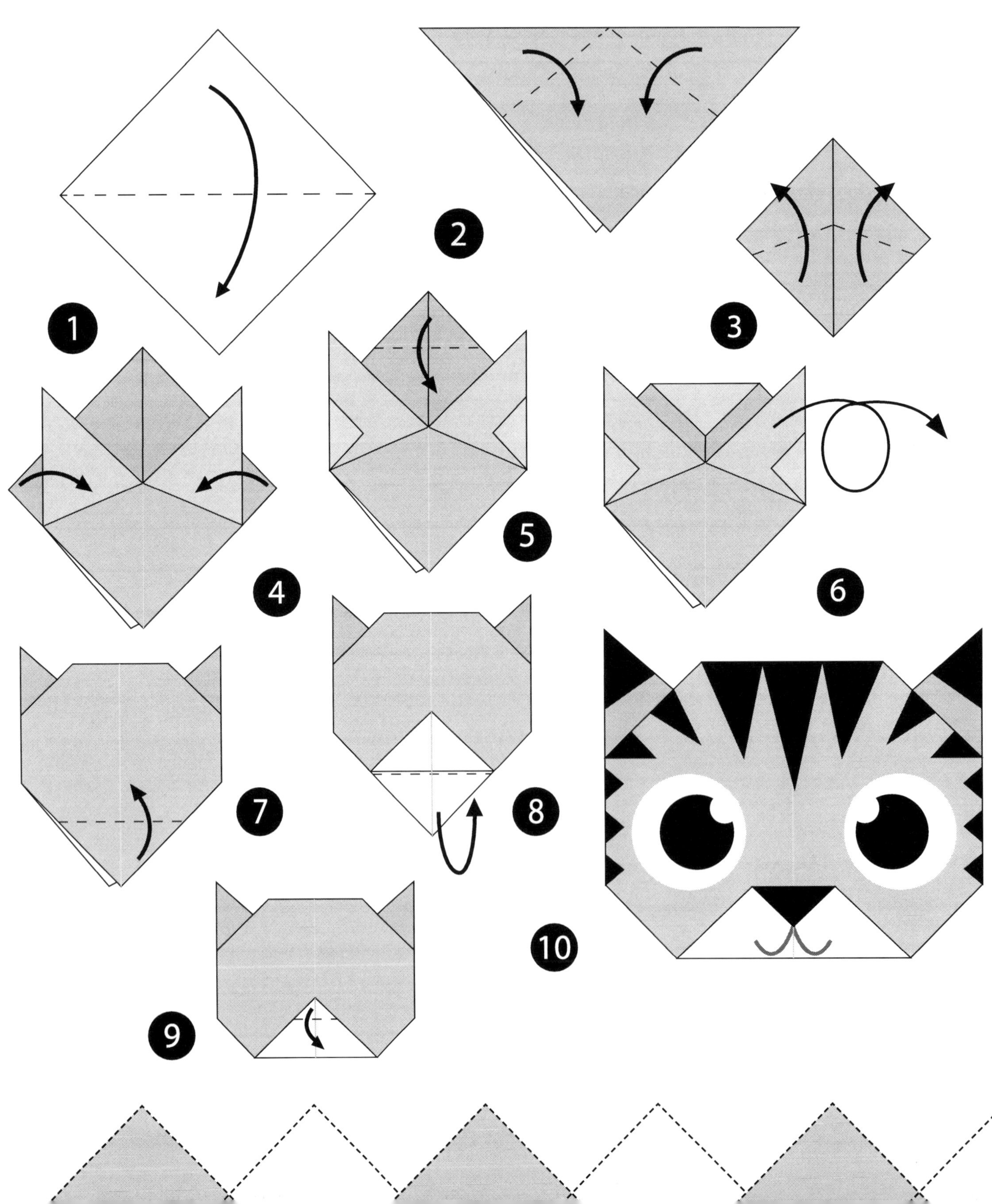

Frog

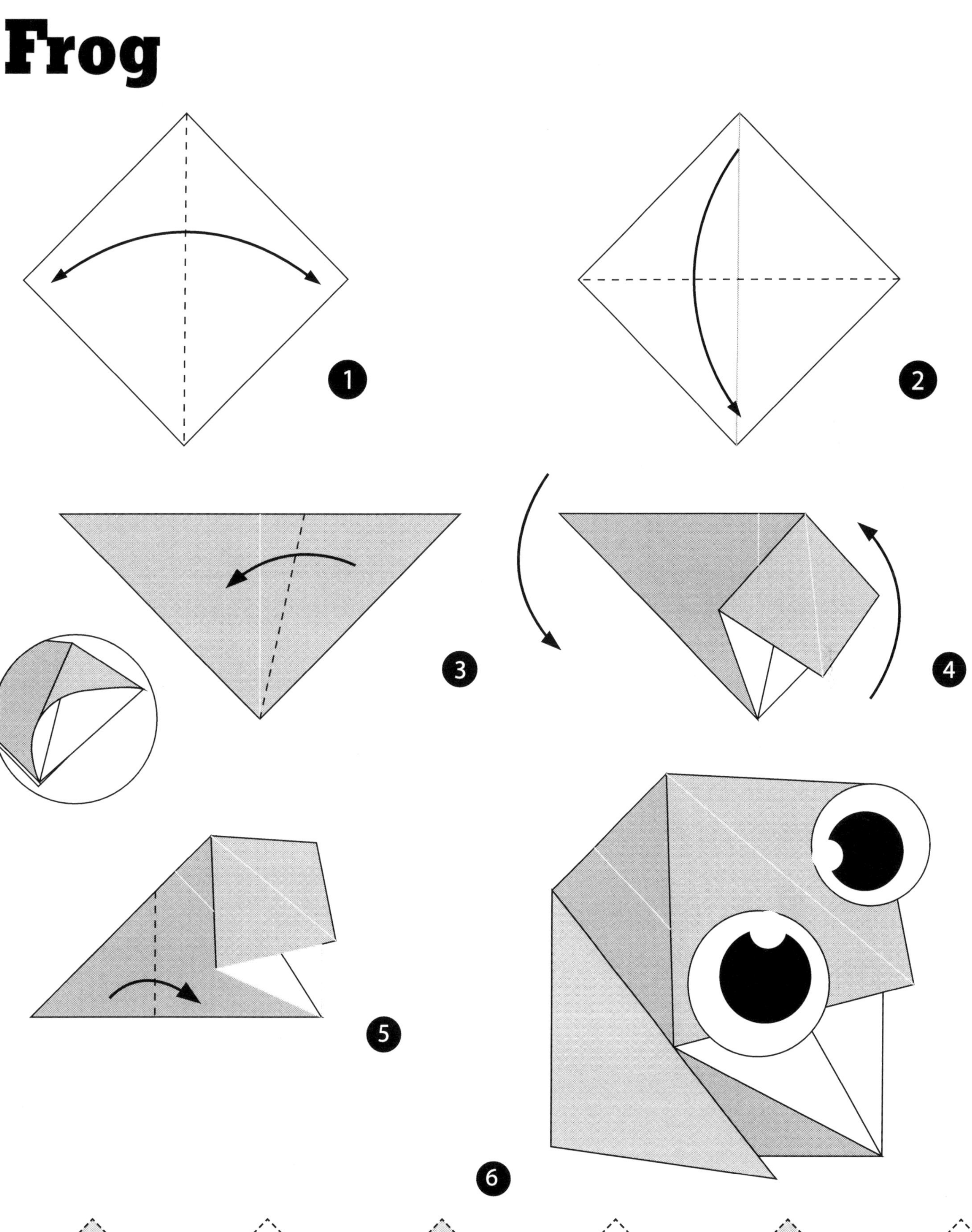

Panda

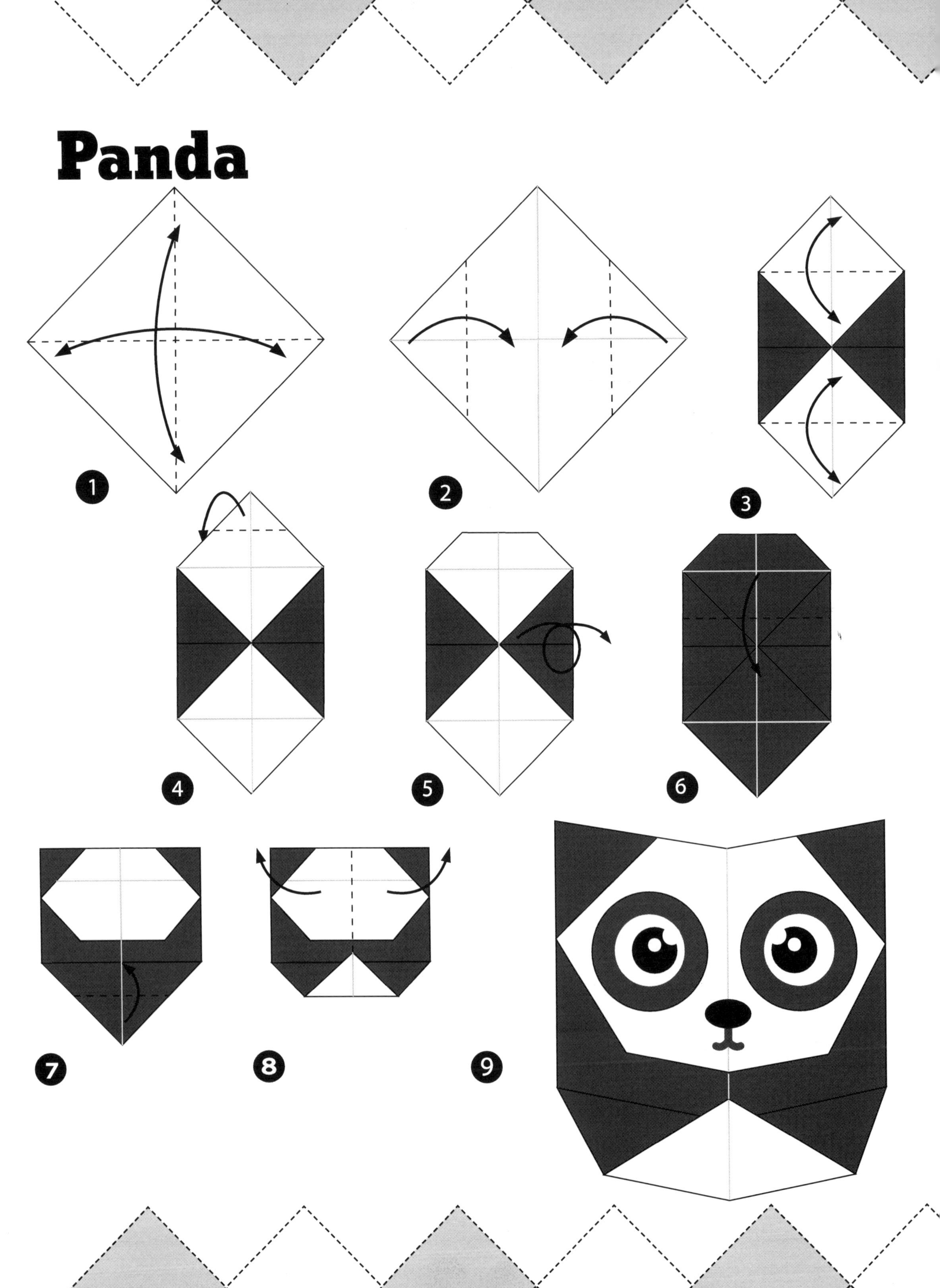

Dog in a Boat

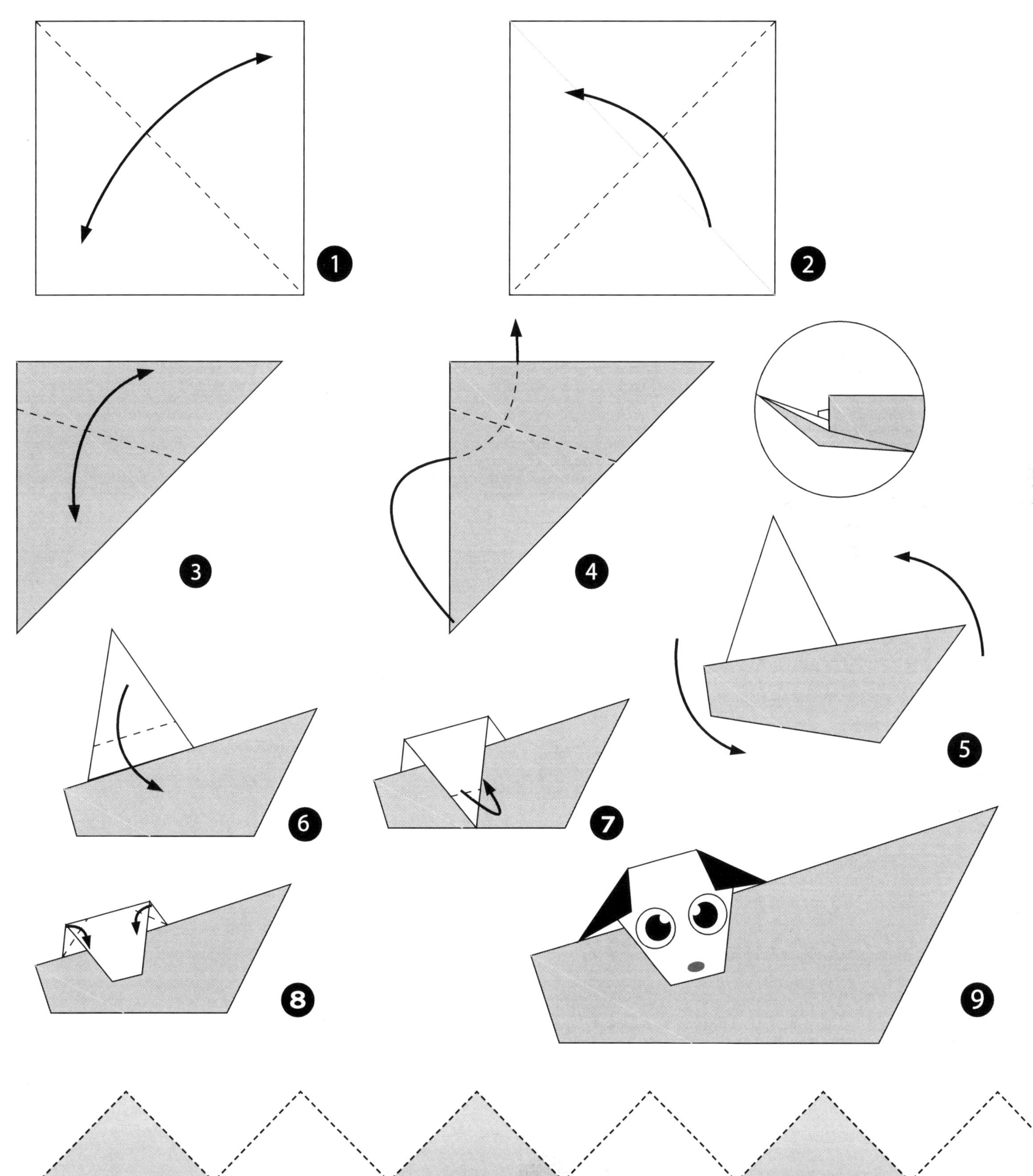

Windmill

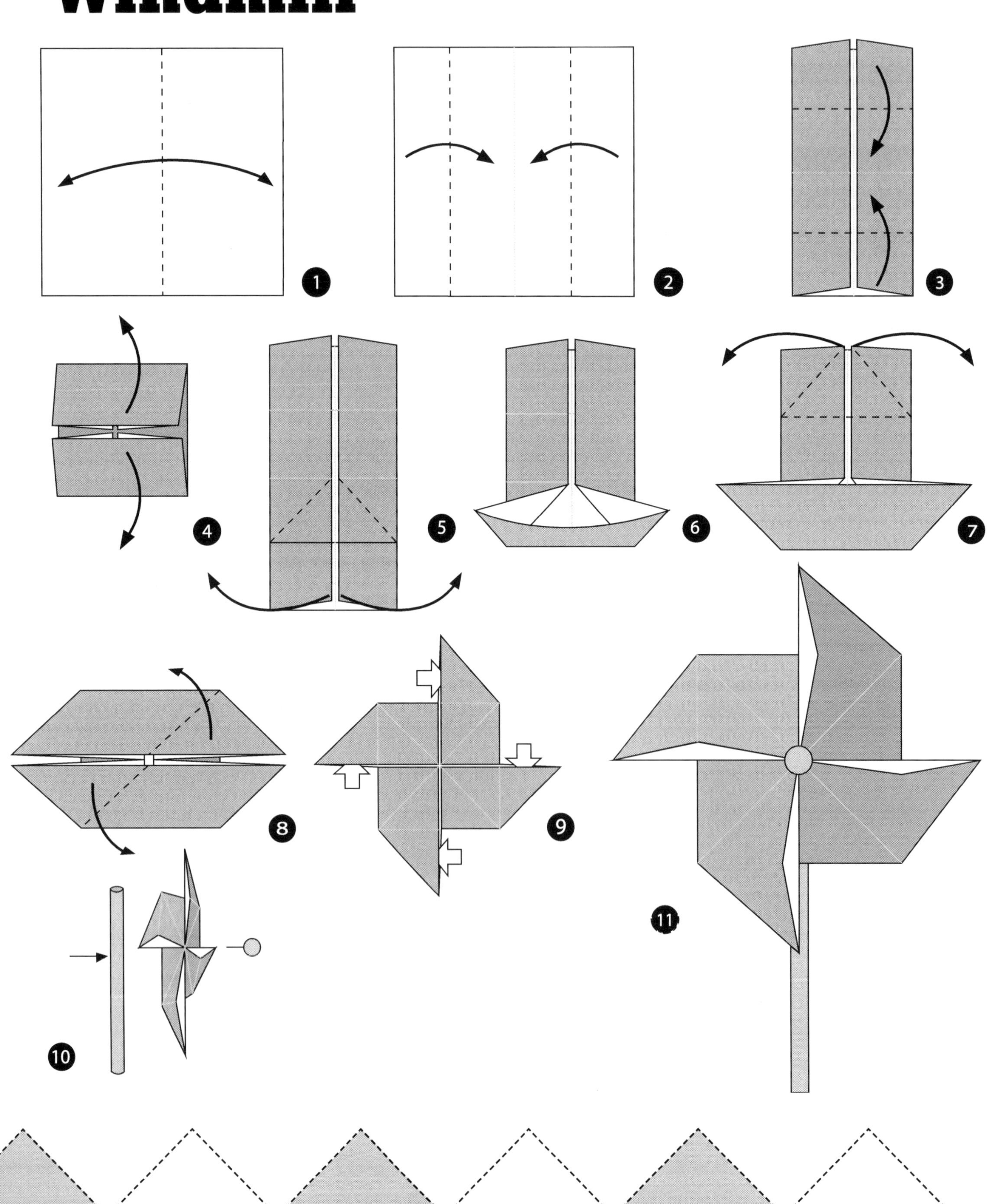

Doggie

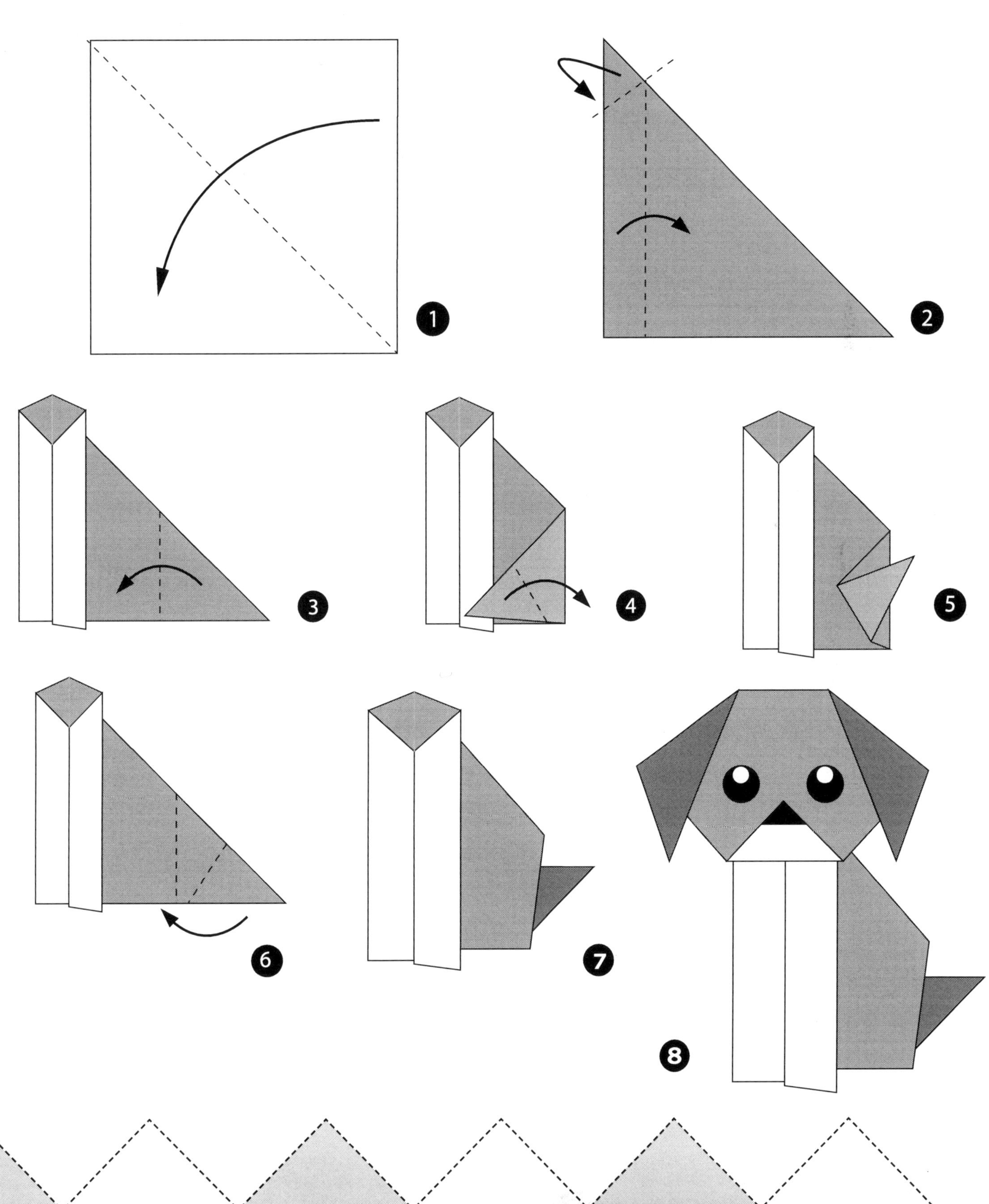

Fox

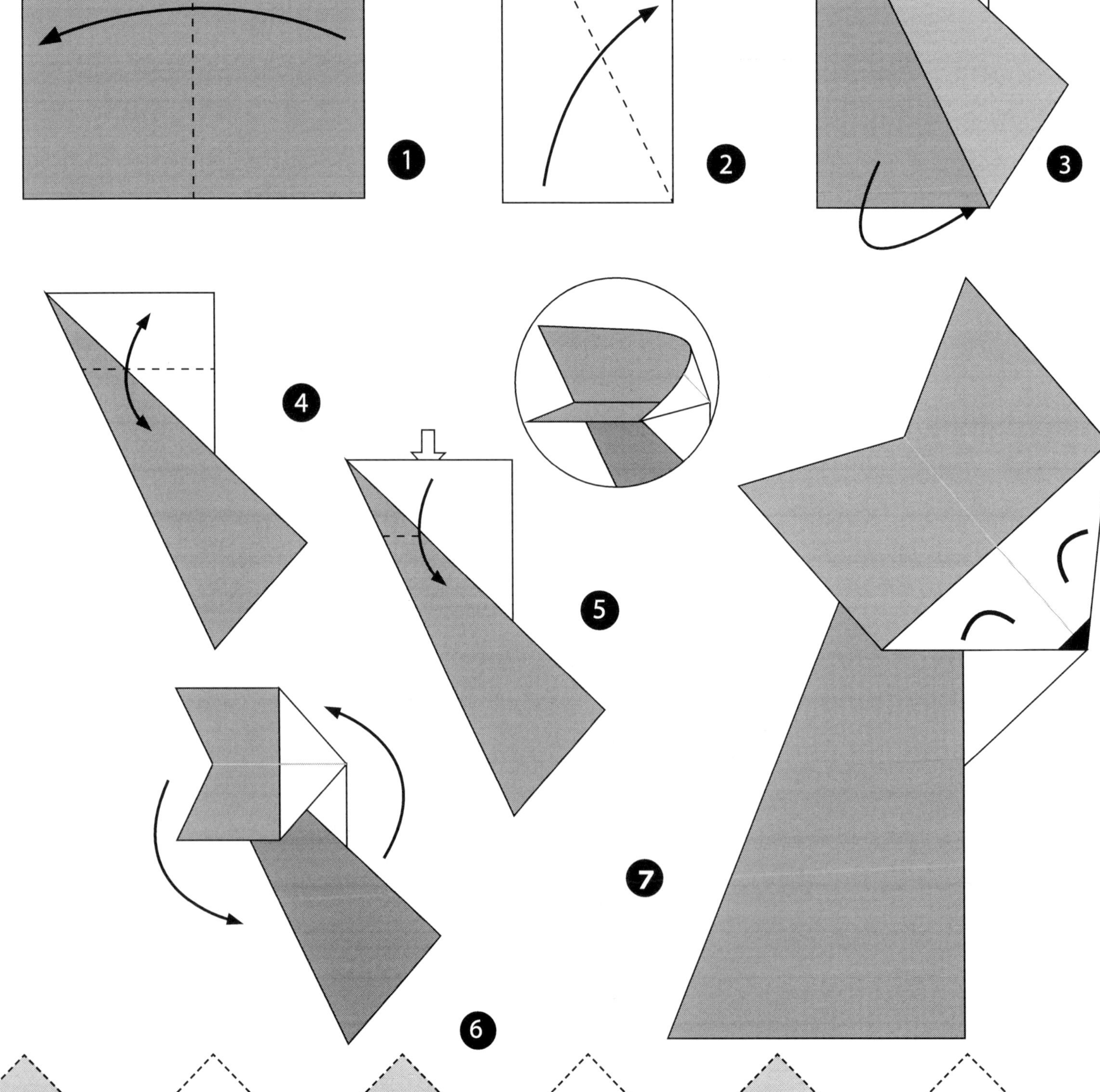

Origami Papers

Each project in this book starts with a square of paper. Cut out the square you like for each project!

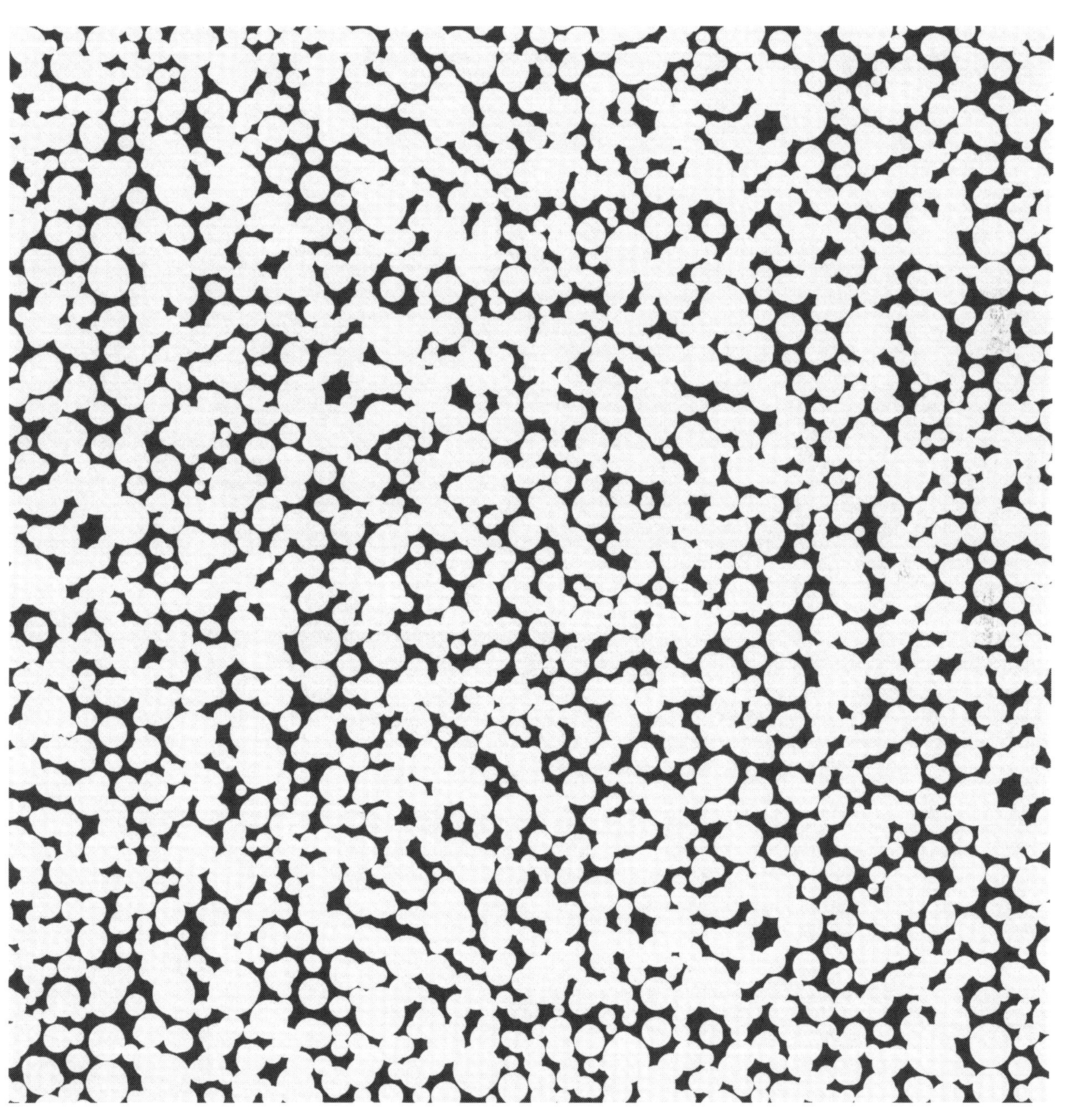

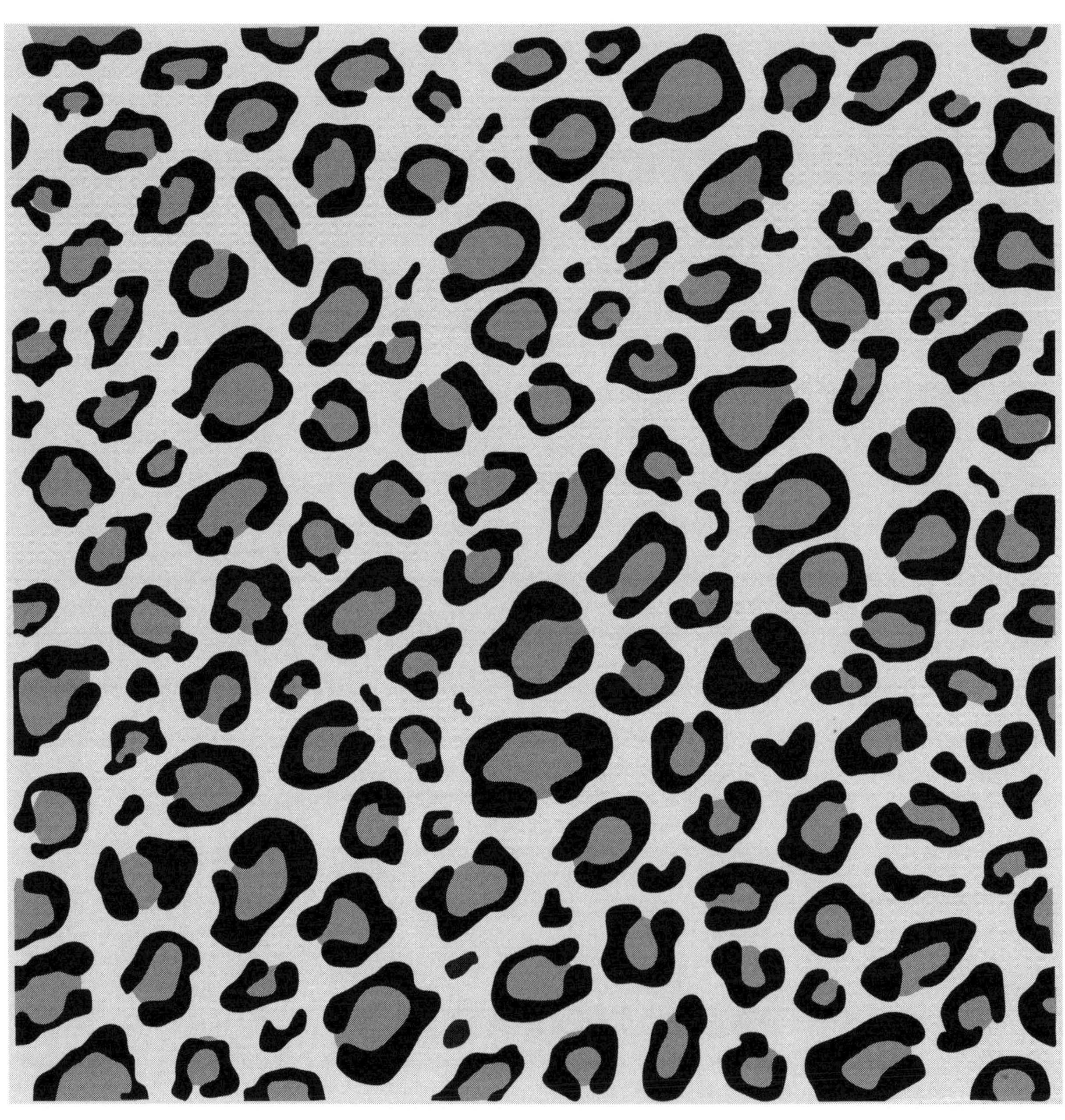

Eyes!

Cut out and use these fun eyes on your finished projects!

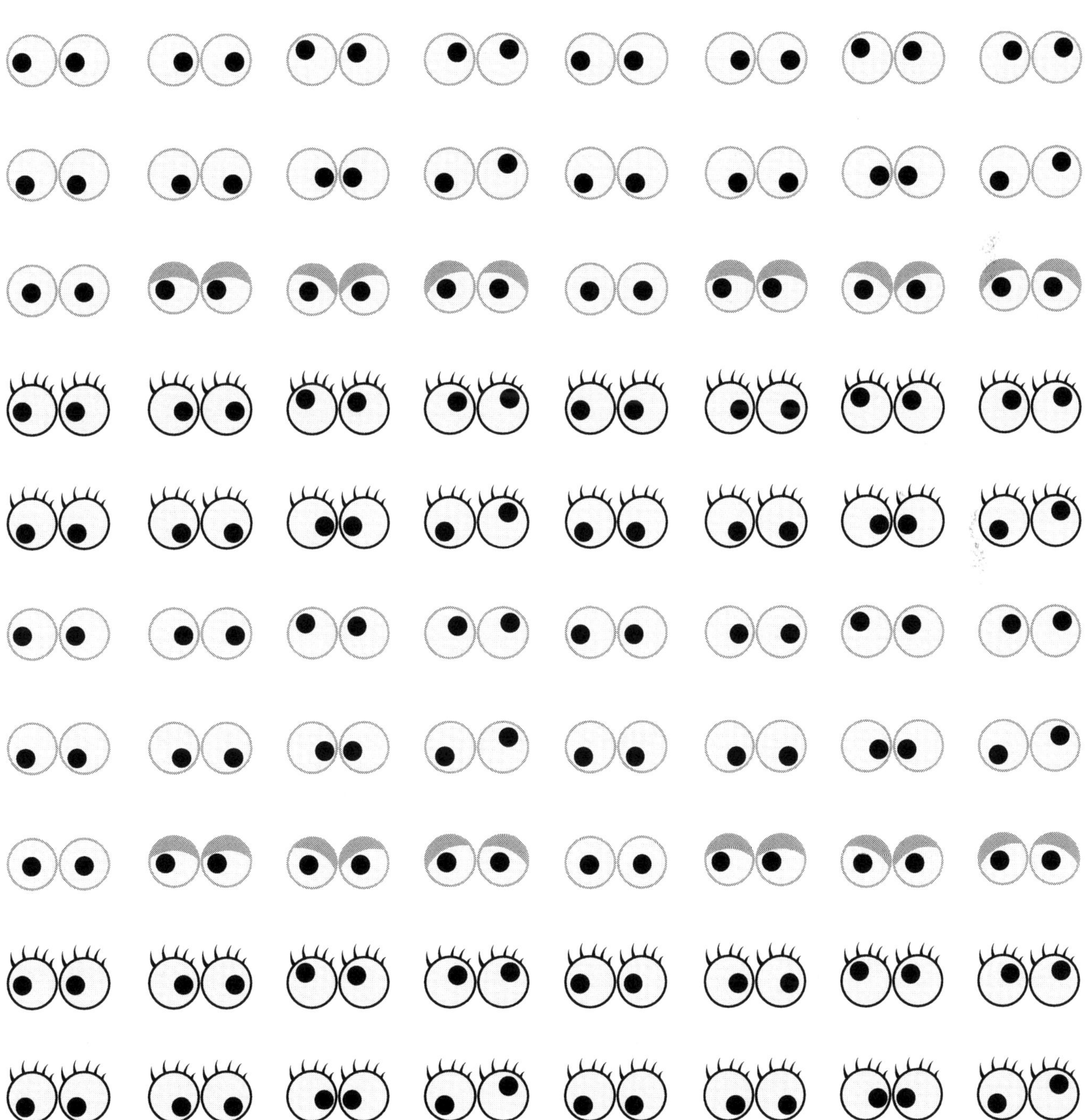

Faces!

Cut out and use these fun animal features on your finished projects!

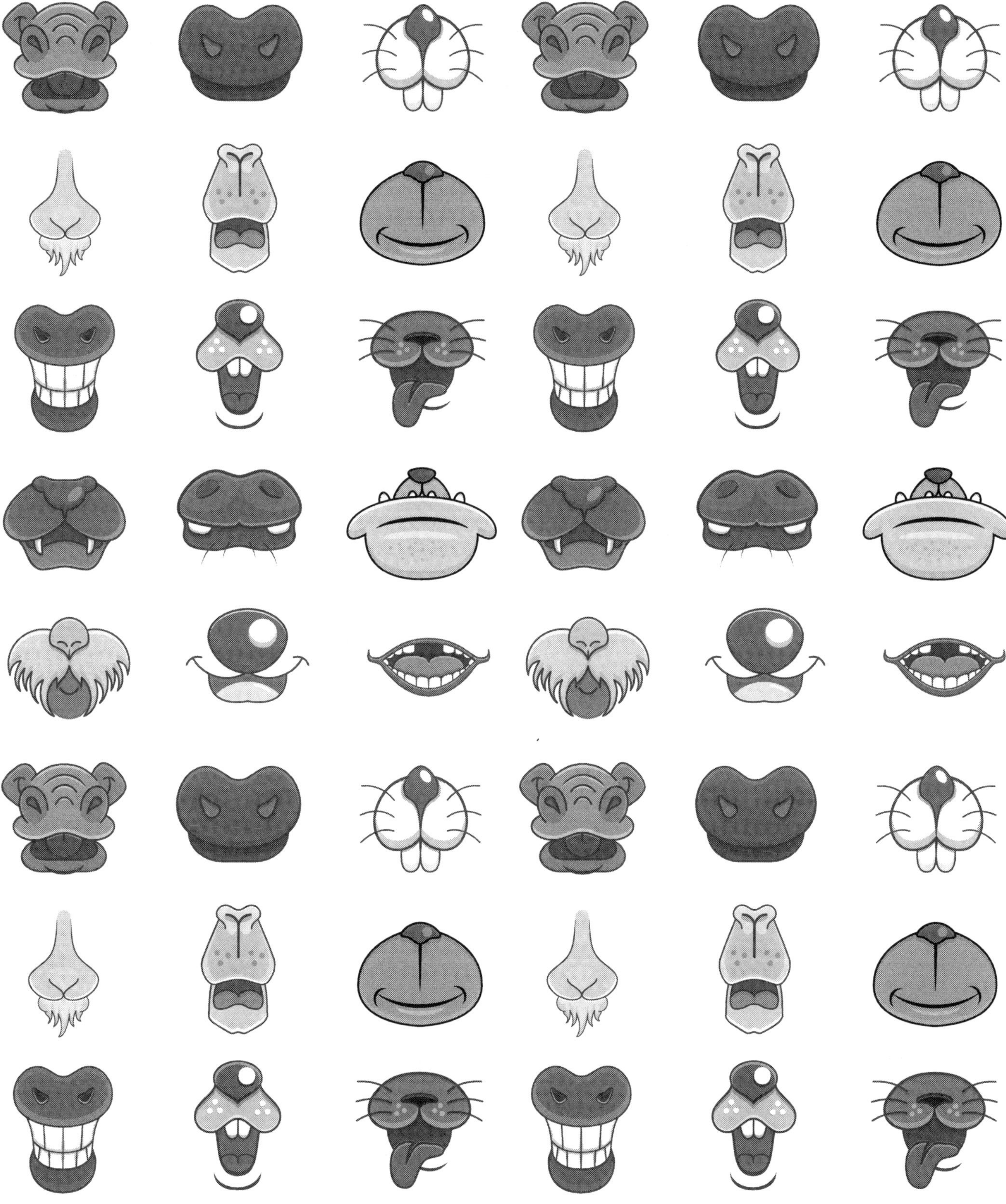

Made in the USA
San Bernardino, CA
19 May 2019